Justices of the Supreme Court

ROGER TANEY

The Dred Scott Legacy

Suzanne Freedman

ENSLOW PUBLISHERS, INC.

44 Fadem Rd.   P.O. Box 38

Box 699   Aldershot

Springfield, NJ 07081   Hants GU12 6BP

U.S.A.   U.K.

Dedication

To Carole, Ellen, and Allan
who consistently make me proud to be their mother

Copyright © 1995 by Suzanne Freedman

Library of Congress Cataloging-in-Publication Data

Freedman, Suzanne, 1932-
    Roger Taney: The Dred Scott Legacy/Suzanne Freedman.
       p. cm. — (Justices of the Supreme Court)
    Includes bibliographical references and index.
    ISBN 0-89490-560-0
    1. United States. Supreme Court—History—Juvenile literature. 2. Judges—United
States—Biography—Juvenile literature. 3. Scott, Dred, 1809-1858—Juvenile literature.
4. Salvery—Law and legislation—United States—Juvenile literature. I. Title. II. Series.
KF8745.T3F74   1995
347.73'2634—dc20
[B]
[347.30733534]
[B]   94-30953
                                   CIP

Printed in the United States of America

10 9 8 7 6 5 4 3 2 1

Photo Credits: Architect of the Capitol, pp. 7, 11; Collection of the Supreme Court of the
United States, pp. 49, 52, 55, 68, 77; Reproduced from the collections of the Library of
Congress, pp. 13, 20, 23, 33, 37; Senate Collection, p. 9; Suzanne Freedman, pp. 27, 29, 74,
82, 87

Cover Photo: Vic Boswell, "Collection of the Supreme Court of the United States."

CONTENTS

1

"It Is the Judgment of This Court . . ."

Roger Brooke Taney, Chief Justice of the United States, put on the long black robe that was hanging on a hook in the Robing Room right next to the Supreme Court chamber. Then he walked slowly to the center seat on the bench. He was followed by the Associate Justices, who sat either to his left or to his right according to how many years they had served on the Court. The Taney Court had been "sitting" in this small chamber on the first floor of the old Capitol building since 1836, when Taney was appointed Chief Justice.

Judges, lawyers, and reporters continually criticized the room. A leading New York newspaperman had once described it as a "queer room . . . shaped overhead like a quarter section of a pumpkin shell . . . a dark, damp, low, subterranean apartment."[1]

Facing the bench is a plaster relief of the figure of "Lady Justice," who is holding scales in her left hand, while her right hand rests on an unsheathed sword. At her feet an eagle guards four volumes of law books. To Lady Justice's right sits a winged youth, the rising sun behind him indicating a new nation. He is holding a large tablet that represents the Constitution of the United States.

In the foreground of the small room were four mahogany counsel tables covered in green on which were placed oil-burning lamps. On the raised platform, in front of the red-curtained windows, were nine mahogany desks at which the Justices sat. To one side of them sat Deputy Clerk D. W. Middleton, Clerk William T. Carroll, and Attorney General Caleb Cushing. To the Justices' left, at the other end, sat Deputy Marshal Philips, Marshal Hoover, and the official court reporter Benjamin C. Howard.

Former Chief Justice John Marshall's portrait hung on one wall nearly up to the ceiling. Rich carpets and silk drapes gave the room a dignified atmosphere. The smallness of the quarters seemed to make the Justices appear larger and more powerful than they actually were.

Roger Brooke Taney (pronounced *Taw' ney*) was completely devoted to the Supreme Court. The United States Constitution was his standard. He put the law above everything else, even if it offended his moral judgment. He had "a first-rate legal mind, and was a clear, forceful writer . . . [H]e realized that constitutional law required vision and common sense as well as careful legal analysis . . . to find in the United States Constitution the necessary authority for states to solve their own problems . . ."[2]

Taney was a tall man with square shoulders who tended to stoop. He had "a face without one good feature, a mouth

This is how the old Supreme Court chamber looked when Roger Taney was its Chief Justice. At the top of the photo you can see the ceiling shaped like a quarter section of a pumpkin shell.

unusually large, in which were discolored and irregular teeth, the gums of which were visible when he smiled, dressed always in black, his clothes sitting ill upon him, his hands spare with projecting veins . . . a gaunt, ungainly man. And yet, when he began to speak you never thought of his personal appearance, so clear . . . were his low-voiced words. He used no gestures. . . . There was an air of so much sincerity in all he said. . . . Not a redundant syllable, not a phrase repeated and . . . so exquisitely simple."[3]

On the second Monday of the December term of 1856, at a few minutes after eleven in the morning, the Taney Court was sitting in the chilly courtroom, heated only by fireplaces.[4] Dred Scott's attorney, Montgomery Blair, was presenting his client's side of the case before the Court. A slave for over forty years, Scott now wanted his freedom. Attorneys Henry S. Geyer and Reverdy Johnson argued for their client, John Sanford, who wanted Scott to remain his "property."

The attorneys could barely see the faces of the nine Justices, who sat with their backs to the natural light that entered only from the three rear windows. The Chief Justice listened intently to the oral arguments for both sides, his quill pen in hand, taking notes. Days passed. Finally, the attorneys finished. The Justices then adjourned to the nearby conference room.

The Chief Justice always presided over the conference room, where the Justices isolated themselves to review and discuss each case as it had been presented. As Chief Justice, Taney would state the facts as well as the arguments and conclusions. Then he would invite the other Justices to discuss and argue amongst themselves. The discussions were usually free and open until everyone was satisfied. Then each Justice would give reasons for his conclusions.

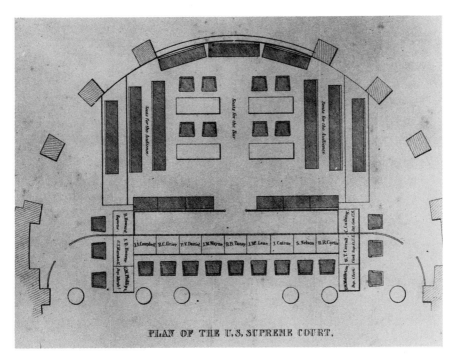

PLAN OF THE U.S. SUPREME COURT.

This floor plan of the United States Supreme Court shows the layout of the courtroom. When the Justices would isolate themselves to review a case, sometimes they would meet in the boarding houses where they lived.

But this time, they simply could not agree. They were too far apart on the issues. On one occasion, in the midst of a heated discussion in the conference room when the Justices were arguing and waving their hands about, Taney snapped, "Brothers, this is the Supreme Court of the United States. Take your seats."[5] It was then that Associate Justice Samuel Nelson suggested that they postpone a decision until after the November election.

Little notice of the *Dred Scott* case had appeared in the newspapers anyway. The nation was too preoccupied with the presidential campaign of 1856. At their convention, the Democrats had picked former Secretary of State and one-time Minister to Great Britain, James "Old Buc" Buchanan of Pennsylvania as their candidate. He was nominated over President Franklin Pierce on the seventeenth ballot.

The Democrats wanted a candidate who would run on a platform pledging to the nation "non-interference by Congress with slavery in state and territory."[6] The Republicans nominated former United States Senator John C. Frémont. Buchanan won by almost half a million popular votes and became the nation's fifteenth president. (Buchanan had been Taney's personal favorite. They had much in common: both were alumni of Dickinson College, successful lawyers, and loyal Democrats. And both opposed slavery in principle but defended it under the Constitution.)

"Poor, foolish Buchanan! He had hoped for a peaceful term of office."[7] With the election now over, the nation was awaiting the Supreme Court decision on the *Dred Scott* case. Justice John Catron, in what today would be considered an error in judicial conduct, wrote to President Buchanan urging him to persuade Justice Robert Grier to join with the majority opinion in the *Dred Scott* case. Grier, who had been

Opposite the bench where the nine Justices sat was a plaster relief of *Justice* by Carlo Franzoni (1817). It shows Justice, an eagle guarding law books, and a winged youth holding a large tablet representing the United States Constitution.

undecided on one of the issues, changed his opinion after talking it over with Buchanan, promising the president he would vote with Taney.

After the final discussions and debates in the conference room, seven of the nine Justices now agreed on a decision. Justices John McLean and Benjamin Curtis did not agree, but the majority had it! Taney was asked to write the opinion and he willingly assumed the task. He went home to begin writing it so that it would be finished a few days after Buchanan's inauguration.

March 4, 1857, Inauguration Day, was an unusually mild and clear day in Washington, D.C.[8] Tens of thousands of spectators arrived on special trains, stagecoaches, carriages, and on horseback for the occasion. Some paid fifty cents to camp out on cots in a circus tent erected especially for the inaugural. Outgoing President Franklin Pierce, almost forgotten in the gala goings-on, and President-elect Buchanan shared an open carriage just behind the brass bands and a float bearing the goddess of liberty. On their arrival at the East Wing of the Capitol, they were met by Vice President-elect John Breckenridge of Kentucky. They all then proceeded to the platform, which had been specially built over the Capitol steps.

Chief Justice Taney administered the oath of office to James Buchanan, who was "dressed in black, fortified with brandy . . . loudly cheered."[9] Buchanan slipped this clause into his inaugural address:

> Slavery . . . is a judicial question which . . . belongs to the Supreme Court of the United States, before whom it . . . will . . . be speedily and finally settled. To their decision, I shall cheerfully submit whatever this may be. . . .[10]

This watercolor by William R. Birch is of the newly constructed Senate wing of the capitol around 1800.

Horace Greeley, founder and editor of the *New York Daily Tribune* and an antislavery supporter, wrote this editorial the following day:

> You may "cheerfully submit" to whatever the five slaveholders and two or three doughfaces on the bench of the Supreme Court may be ready to utter on this subject.[11] But not one man who really desires the triumph of freedom over Slavery in the territories will do so. . . .[12]

Taney, now almost eighty years of age, arose early on the morning of March 6. The inauguration two days earlier had exhausted him. But he did not want to miss morning Mass at the Cathedral of the Assumption. After the church service, he walked the few short blocks to the Capitol, his papers tucked snugly under his arm. He slowly climbed up the Senate staircase and made his way toward the courtroom.

The large clock Taney had ordered for the courtroom struck eleven. In the small Robing Room, the nine Justices put on their long black robes. Court Clerk William Carroll cried, "Oyez" ("Hear Ye"). The spectators rose to their feet. Chief Justice Taney entered, followed by the eight Associate Justices. They proceeded to the "bench," each taking his seat. Taney sat in the center in a winged mahogany chair. He signaled to the clerk who shouted again, "Oyez, oyez, oyez! All persons having business before the Honorable, the Supreme Court of the United States, are admonished to draw near and give their attention, for the Court is now sitting. God save the United States and this Honorable Court."[13]

The available wood "love seats" and upholstered sectional sofas just barely accommodated the lawyers and law students prepared to take notes, the newspaper reporters anxious to release the latest news to their readers, "the gay ladies in their

14

waving plumes, and the members of either house that stepped in to listen."[14] Everyone there seemed to sense that something important was about to happen. They had come to hear Chief Justice Taney read the Court's opinion and to learn the fate of Dred Scott and his family. The crowd waited for Taney to begin. He cleared his throat. His hands trembled as he picked up the fifty-five page manuscript.

His voice sounded feeble but his words were strong. He summed up the facts on the *Dred Scott* case, and then said:

> It is not the province of the Court to decide upon the justice or injustice, the policy or impolicy of these laws. The decision of that question belonged to the political or lawmaking power; to those who . . . framed the Constitution. The duty of the Court is to interpret the instrument they have framed . . . according to its true intent and meaning when it was adopted."[15]

His voice almost dropped to a whisper. His shoulders sagged. His blue eyes seemed to recede into his wrinkled face. He continued:

> but there are two clauses in the Constitution which point directly . . . to the Negro[16] race as a separate class of persons, and show clearly that they were not regarded as . . . citizens of the government then formed . . . it is obvious that they were not even in the minds of the framers of the Constitution when they were conferring special rights and privileges upon the citizens of a state in every other part of the Union."[17]

The abolitionists, those who were opposed to slavery, suspected that their hopes for a decision favorable to their cause were doomed. This will certainly be tomorrow's headlines. The young law students could hardly wait to record the highlights of the Court's opinion.

Chief Justice Taney was coming to the end of his reading. More than two hours had passed. There was complete silence in the courtroom. He concluded, "Upon the whole, therefore, it is the judgment of this Court. . . ."[18]

"Such Is Ambition in the Little World and the Great . . ."

At the top of a rolling slope in the western part of Calvert County in southern Maryland stood the tobacco plantation where Roger Brooke Taney was born. Tall trees surrounded the three-story house that looked down on the Patuxent River.

Taney was born on St. Patrick's Day, March 17, 1777. The American colonies were uniting to become independent of England. The Declaration of Independence had been signed one year earlier, but the United States Constitution was not to be adopted for another ten years.

Roger Taney was descended from an English Catholic family that had settled in Maryland around 1660. The Taney family had purchased land and had become very successful planting tobacco in the fertile soil of Maryland's rolling hills. The estate was eventually left to Michael Taney, Roger's father, who carried on the family tradition of an aristocratic southern gentleman.

At that time, wealthy Southerners invested in Negroes who would become their slaves for life. Slaves would perform tasks on the Taney tobacco plantation directed and managed by Taney's father, a typical Southern slave owner. Even with the trade restrictions that had hurt the sale of tobacco, the Taneys somehow managed to keep their land and their slaves.

Michael and Monica Brooke Taney had four sons and three daughters. Roger was their third child and second son. The children were raised as Catholics. Taney's father was "physically strong, hot-tempered, impatient and arrogant."[1] In later years, Roger would describe his mother Monica as "pious, affectionate . . . when any of us . . . committed a fault, her reproof was gentle. . . . I remember and feel the effect of her teaching to this hour."[2]

Roger Taney was a combination of his mother and father. He was impulsive like his father but had the gentle and loving disposition of his mother. Michael Taney took pleasure in teaching his sons to ride, swim, and fish, to row and sail in summer, to shoot ducks and wild geese in winter. From his father, Roger came to appreciate the pleasures of the countryside. He loved riding. Although his health was not good, he rode as hard as anyone and eagerly followed the hounds. Roger became an enthusiastic fox-hunter. But most of all, he liked to just sit beside a quiet stream on a hillside reading or daydreaming.

"It was no part of my father's plan to give my elder brother a classical education. He was strongly imbued with . . . perpetuating the family estate in the eldest son . . . his younger sons would have a liberal education and the means of studying a profession."[3]

For some years, Roger and his older brother and sister attended school in a log cabin about three miles from home. Here they learned to read. "The bible . . . was used mainly as a book to teach us how to spell words and pronounce them."[4] Roger said.

When their teacher became mentally ill, the children were taught at home by tutors. Roger's tutor, Princeton-educated David English, thought so highly of Roger's ability that he advised Michael Taney to send Roger to college, even though he was then only fifteen. "My father was induced to select Dickinson College from the circumstance that two young men, a few years older . . . were already there, with whose families he was intimately acquainted and who gave very favorable accounts of the institution."[5]

Dickinson College in Carlisle, Pennsylvania, was founded in 1783 and named for Governor John Dickinson. Roger Taney's journey there in 1792 was his first time away from home. He packed his trunk with a year's supply of clothes. The journey to Carlisle was a challenge for the slender, frail boy. "It was no small undertaking . . . to get from the lower part of Calvert County to Carlisle,"[6] Roger remembered.

One of the neighborhood boys accompanied Roger on his journey, which began on the boat landing on the Patuxent River just below his home. The boys boarded a merchant ship filled with a cargo of farm produce. The ship sailed down the river to the Chesapeake Bay and up the bay to Baltimore. The trip took about a week because of unfavorable winds. Once in Baltimore, they had to stay at an inn until they could find a wagon big enough to carry them and their trunks to Carlisle.

Taney did not catch his first glimpse of Carlisle until a week later. The trip had taken two weeks altogether and was so difficult that Roger only went home twice in the three

The Taney family home overlooked the Patuxent River in Calvert County, Maryland. Roger Taney, his older brother, and his sister all went to school in a log cabin about three miles from their childhood home.

years he attended Dickinson. Both times he and a classmate actually *walked* from Carlisle to Baltimore (a two-day journey of about eighty-five miles!)

Dickinson consisted of a plain two-story building; ". . . small and shabby . . . fronting on a dirty alley."[7] The small building accommodated sixty-five students and professors, three classrooms, and a library.

The homesick fifteen-year-old country boy was taken under the wing of fifty-six-year-old Dr. Charles Nisbet, a man "stoutly built . . . in ministerial black, sharp nose, and bright eyes under a full white powdered wig."[8] Dr. Nisbet became Roger's guardian in the absence of his father.

Taney learned logic and moral philosophy from Nisbet, and geography and history from Dr. Robert Davidson. There were no courses in modern languages, not even English grammar. Charles Huston, a young law student, taught him Latin and Greek.

Huston noticed that Roger was ahead of his classmates, that he was "unusually bright" and suggested that "[he] be put in a special class . . . and thus be given an opportunity by hard work to catch up with the members of the junior class."[9]

In looking back at his college years, Taney recalled that "under these professors [Davidson, Huston, Nisbet] . . . I studied closely, was always well prepared in my lessons, and, while I gladly joined my companions in their athletic sports and activities, I yet found time to read a great deal beyond the books we were required to study."[10]

Taney was elected valedictorian of the class of 1795, for which he had to write a speech. Never having taken an English grammar course, he found it difficult. "It was to be submitted to Dr. Nisbet before it was delivered . . . and I feared he might find it all wrong . . . I had never written a paragraph of my own composition, except familiar . . . letters to my family."[11]

"This oration cost me much trouble and anxiety," Taney declared, "I remember well that my greatest difficulty was how to begin it; and the first two or three sentences gave me nearly as much trouble as all the rest of it put together. I am quite sure that I spent hours upon them, and wrote them over at least a dozen times."[12]

The commencement was held in the large Presbyterian church where Dr. Nisbet regularly preached. A large platform was built in front of the pulpit for the occasion.

> I sat on this platform . . . awaiting my turn, thinking over what I had to say, and trying to muster up enough courage to speak it with composure. But I was sadly frightened, and trembled in every limb, and my voice was husky and unmanageable. Fortunately, my speech had been so well committed to memory that I went through without the aid of the prompter.[13]

Taney was to reflect upon that day sixty years later:

> My college honor was of no consequence in my future pursuits. Yet in the little world of a college, it is as much valued, and as much the object of ambition, as the high offices of government in the great political world. And I confess that I would, at that time, have endured much more than I did rather than not have obtained it. Such is ambition in the little world and the great, and so early do our teachers and instructors plant it in our hearts . . .[14]

After graduation, Roger Taney returned to his tree-shaded home on the Patuxent River where he spent the winter of 1795. While his health was not good, he nevertheless managed to enjoy fox-hunting—he rode and eagerly followed

Unlike the tree-shaded home on the Patuxent river, Roger Taney spent the latter part of his young adult life at the this house in Frederick, Maryland.

the hounds. By winter's end he had become a confirmed fox-hunter. But he soon tired of this idle life. He was impatient to begin the study of law. He said: "It was the profession my father had always desired me to follow, and which I myself preferred."[15]

Taney studied law in the spring of 1796 in Annapolis with Judge Jeremiah Townley Chase, a judge of the General Court of Maryland. Taney didn't have an active social life and "for weeks together [he] read law twelve hours of the twenty-four."[16]

Francis Scott Key, a fellow law student, and the man who would write *The Star Spangled Banner*, also began his studies there a few months after Taney. They became fast friends. Key would invite Taney to visit Terra Rubra (meaning "red earth"), the Keys' ancestral home and one of the largest mansions in Maryland. It had been built by Francis's grandfather. Key introduced Taney to his sister Anne who was then about sixteen years old. Seven years later, Anne would become Taney's wife.

Taney was admitted to the Annapolis bar in the spring of 1799.[17] He was twenty-two years old. (Soon afterward, he was elected a member of the Maryland House of Delegates [part of the State Legislature] for a two-year term.) From the beginning public speaking was a problem for him and it continued to cause him a lot of embarrassing moments throughout his life: "I feared that I should break down in my first essay at the Bar," Taney declared. "I knew I must be able to think and exercise the power of reasoning while I was speaking, and while I was conscious that everyone was looking at me and listening to me."[18]

Purposely, he chose a simple case his first time out. It involved the defense of a man indicted on an assault and battery charge. Taney argued the case in a local court in Annapolis.

> I took no notes, for my hand shook so that I could not have written a word legibly if my life had depended on it; and when I rose to speak, I was obliged to fold my arms over my breast, pressing them firmly against my body; and my knees trembled under me so much that I was obliged to press my limbs against the table before me to keep me steady on my feet . . . [19]

The verdict in favor of Taney's client hardly consoled him. Despite that encouragement it was a constant struggle to keep his nerves in check. He tried to master his feelings of stagefright when he made his first speech in the Maryland Court of Appeals and when he first appeared before the Supreme Court. But because of his nervousness, he usually did not make any public speeches.

Taney almost abandoned the practice of law because of these feelings. But he needed the money to live on. He also felt he could not disappoint his father and the rest of his family who had helped pay for his education and who had high hopes for his future. [20]

Taney's strong will and determination helped him overcome his fears and other difficulties. His health was delicate, and court proceedings, which sometimes lasted two or three weeks, completely exhausted him. But, in spite of this, he managed to enter wholeheartedly into law and politics. The discussions in the House of Delegates enabled him gradually to speak with less embarrassment. The debates there allowed him to associate with distinguished men, thus giving him more confidence.

He was defeated for a second term in the House of Delegates. That put an end to any prospects for political office for the time being. "My father and myself . . . were sufficiently mortified at this defeat . . . ," Taney declared, "and as it never had been intended that Calvert should be my permanent place of residence, there was no object to be gained by continuing there any longer."[21]

Michael Taney and his son talked about where Roger ought to start a law practice. Michael suggested Baltimore, a major port with a population of 26,000 people and the largest city in Maryland.

But just as friendship had been the reason for his choice of Dickinson College, so did friendship influence his decision about where to practice law. "I therefore proposed Frederick . . . next to Annapolis and Baltimore, it was, with a view to profit, the best place of practice in the state. . . . I had at Annapolis formed friendships with some young men near my own age who resided in Frederick. And I felt that I should not . . . be as lonely and without friends, on my first arrival, as I should have been in Baltimore."[22]

Key, one of Taney's closest friends, was certainly a strong influence in his decision to settle in Frederick. Key spoke of the town as a place of rapid development and enterprise. There were many prosperous landowners and at least eighty gristmills grinding wheat into flour. Frederick was also surrounded by iron furnaces, glass factories, paper mills, marble quarries, banks, grocery stores, hardware stores, print shops, and tanneries.

Taney moved to this growing town of about three thousand in March of 1801 and was admitted to the Frederick bar that same month. He soon set up a law office with Key, who had been admitted to the bar three days after

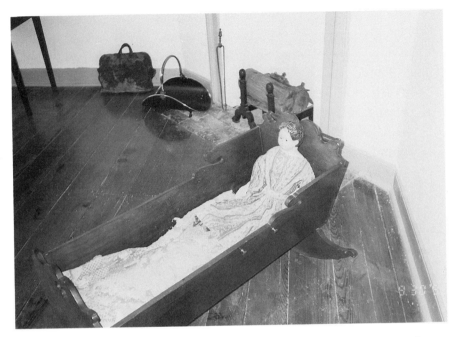

This wooden cradle was used by Roger Taney's daughters. It is now part of the exhibit at the Taney House in Frederick, Maryland.

Taney. Their successful law practice partnership lasted for five years until Key decided to move to Washington, D.C. Taney by this time had become a successful lawyer. He felt he would now be able to support a wife. Taney's choice was Anne Phebe Charlton Key whose "beauty and bright mind and womanly graces won his heart."[23] It was said that Anne reminded him of his mother. He had traveled many times to Terra Rubra to see Anne and now he went there to propose marriage. She accepted and the wedding took place on Tuesday evening, January 7, 1806, before a Catholic priest, Father Nicholas Zocchi.

The Key's drawing room was the setting for the happy occasion. The fireplace was blazing, adding warmth to the chilly evening. Holly and other Christmas greenery added beauty to the scene and candlelight cast shadows about the spacious room. Anne was twenty-two, her groom twenty-nine. Roger, over six feet tall, and Anne, below average in height, made a striking contrast! People described the couple "like the union of a hawk with a skylark."[24]

Anne, raised Episcopalian, and Roger, raised Catholic, agreed that any sons born to them would be raised Catholic, and any daughters Episcopalian. The Taneys had six daughters; their only son died at the age of three.

Religion was rarely discussed in the Taney home. However, Anne was supportive of Roger's religion. She encouraged her daughters to attend Mass and Vespers with their father, who was a very devout Catholic. Their daughter Sophia converted to Catholicism as an adult.

Because of their different religions, Roger Taney, the first Catholic Supreme Court Justice, who died in 1864 at the age of 88, is buried at St. John's Catholic Cemetery, and Anne,

Roger Taney died in 1864 at the age of eighty-eight. He is buried at St. John's Catholic Cemetery in Frederick, MD, along with his mother. His wife who died in the yellow fever epidemic of 1855 is buried in the Mt. Olivet Episcopal Cemetery.

who died in the yellow fever epidemic of 1855, is buried in Mt. Olivet Episcopal Cemetery in Frederick.

The Taney family lived in a modest two-story house on Bentz Street in Frederick, in a "domestic atmosphere of harmony and deep affection."[25] The lovable side of Roger Taney's nature shone through as his otherwise tense and stiff temperament disappeared in the presence of his family.

In the rear of the Taney house there were slave quarters. Roger Taney freed seven young slaves in 1818. He continued to support his older ones by giving them a monthly allowance, always in small silver pieces and never more than fifty cents. Each was given a wallet in which to put his money.

Roger Taney was a devoted citizen of the Frederick community and an honest and able lawyer. His main interest, outside of law, was politics. He became a strong supporter of the colorful and dynamic war hero, Democrat Andrew Jackson.

With his brothers and father now dead, it was left to Roger to give the name of Taney a place in history. At the age of forty-six he was a success, the father of six children, and happily married for over fifteen years.

As he continued to practice law in Frederick, the name Roger Brooke Taney became a familiar one in the community. His reputation had extended to Annapolis, for he argued many court cases there too. But it was to an important urban center that he now directed his ambition—to a city of large estate owners, bankers, and merchants who could afford to pay high legal fees. Taney had, after all, a large family to support. So the Taneys sold the little house on Bentz Street and moved to Baltimore in 1823.

The Road to the Supreme Court

Once in Baltimore, Taney's law practice increased greatly and his sphere of influence broadened. In 1825, after arguing cases in the Court of Appeals and the Federal District Court, Taney appeared for the first time before the United States Supreme Court, the highest court in the land. He still "experienced . . . shattering . . . stage fright."[1]

A colleague once described him as "a man with a moonlight mind, a mind which, like moonlight of the arctics gave all the light of day without its glare."[2] Taney took on all kinds of legal cases and gave every case his best effort. When the arguments were over he would dismiss them from his mind. He felt no further concern about the case, not even any anxiety over the result. Once, when asked about this, he replied: "[I] always do my best in the case, and having done that [I] was not going to worry [my] interiors into fiddlestrings about results."[3]

31

Taney did not win all his cases. After he lost a few, he would lose his temper at the "judges who have decided without taking time to think . . . the argument had been a solemn farce . . ."[4] Taney could not know it then but one day *he* would also be a judge.

In 1827, upon the unanimous recommendation of the Baltimore Bar, Taney was appointed Attorney General of Maryland by Governor Joseph Kent. He was pleased at being the top lawyer in his home state; he had no higher ambition than that. In that capacity, he handled many cases, some involving navigation, business, or commerce of the sea. This was hard for him at first because he had not practiced law in a commercial seaport city like Baltimore, but in a small inland town like Frederick. Taney worked hard, day and night, on all his cases. Then Andrew Jackson was elected President in 1828 and Taney's life began to change. He was about to enter the world of Washington politics.

Taney had never lost his interest in politics, even though it had been many years since he had served in the Maryland State Legislature when he was in his early twenties. His choice for President of the United States was the national hero of the War of 1812 and Democratic Senator from Tennessee, Andrew Jackson. Nicknamed "Old Hickory," Jackson was the favorite to win over John Quincy Adams. Taney started the Jackson party movement in Maryland to elect Jackson and became the chairman of its central committee. Adams was defeated by more than 130,000 popular votes and Andrew Jackson became the seventh President of the United States, a position he held for two terms, until 1836.[5]

Roger Taney was being considered for the cabinet post of Attorney General in the Jackson administration. But he did not want to hold federal office. If he went to Washington,

BORN TO COMMAND.

OF VETO MEMORY.

HAD I BEEN CONSULTED.

KING ANDREW THE FIRST.

This cartoon shows Andrew Jackson, a popular and forceful president, as a monarch who exceeded his authority by vetoing the 1832 bill to recharter the Second Bank of the United States.

D.C. for a four-year term, it would mean losing the substantial income he needed to support his large family.

The only office Taney ever really wanted was the one he held at that time—Attorney General of Maryland. ". . . my family on both the father and mother's side have been for so many generations Maryland people, that I have always felt strong Maryland attachments," he said, "and having no desire for political distinction in power, my highest ambition was to receive the highest bar honor in my native state . . ."[6]

From the beginning, the Jackson administration was surrounded by controversy. Secretary of War John Eaton's wife had been criticized by the other cabinet members and their wives. They did not want to accept her in their social circle since she was, after all, a former barmaid. This affair led to the split between Jackson and his vice-president, John C. Calhoun, whose wife had led the opposition to Peggy O'Neale Eaton. Then other problems developed between Jackson's personal advisers and executive officials.

In the spring of 1831, most of Jackson's cabinet resigned. New cabinet members were appointed. Lewis Cass replaced Eaton as Secretary of War. Edward Livingston replaced Martin Van Buren as Secretary of State. Levi Woodbury became Secretary of the Navy, and Louis McLane was made Secretary of the Treasury. Only William T. Barry kept his position as Postmaster General.

And who would replace John Berrien as Attorney General? Jackson knew of Roger Taney's reputation and he asked Francis Scott Key, Taney's brother-in-law, to find out if Taney would be interested in the cabinet post. Key wrote Taney, "[Jackson] wished to offer you the place of Attorney General. . . . I believed you would accept, because I thought you would feel it a duty. . . . You will find yourself, both as to him [Jackson] and his Cabinet, acting with men who know and value you . . ."[7]

Taney had little or no connection with any government leaders except those within his home state of Maryland. But when a request came from the President of the United States, he felt obliged to honor it. Jackson, a notoriously bad speller, wrote Van Buren: "I have appointed mr Tauney atto. Genl."[8] In July, a local Baltimore paper wrote, ". . . Mr. Taney will be found a safe and firm counsellor and valuable public servant to the state . . . and the Union which receives him may be justly proud."[9]

Taney would find it difficult to recognize his old office today. In 1831, the Attorney General's quarters were simple, with hardly any furniture. His staff consisted of just one clerk and a messenger. (Today, the Attorney General wields great power over thousands of lawyers and other employees.) Attorney General Taney acted as advisor to every bureau of the federal government as well as to President Jackson and other cabinet members. He would charge special fees if he had to represent the government in court cases. Other attorneys described the Attorney General's office as "crushing . . . the most onerous [demanding] in the government and grossly underpaid."[10] Taney's salary was a mere $4,000 a year, equivalent to about $58,000 today.[11]

Jackson often called upon Taney for opinions on a great variety of problems. Despite attempts to solve the problem of Negro rights, the situation had grown more difficult. The North and South were divided as to how to deal with the question of slavery. The South needed slave labor to produce its cotton. The North was using other methods of production that did not include slaves, so the North criticized the South. The Southern states feared and resented the spreading antislavery feelings within their borders and adopted laws "excluding free negroes from other states and from foreign countries, on the ground that they might provoke uprisings among the slaves."[12]

One South Carolina law provided that "free negroes employed on foreign vessels which came into the ports of the state should be seized and held in prison while the vessel was in port."[13] When the ships were ready to leave, the Negroes would be released if the ship's captain paid the prison costs. Otherwise, the Negroes would be sold to recover the costs. A British officer said that the Negroes on his ship were the King's subjects, and that this law was a violation of a treaty between England and the United States.

Secretary of State Livingston asked Taney's opinion about this. "The treaty with Great Britain contained no . . . provision on the subject," Taney declared.

> . . . it was said to be a fixed principle of the law of England that a slave became free as soon as he touched her shores . . . if . . . by the laws of any of the states a slave becomes free, as soon as he is brought within the limits of the state . . . and is there taken by the state authorities from the possession of his owner and declared to be free, the General Government is under no obligation to interfere in behalf of the master, and he has no right to call on the United States to support him in his claim of property.[14]

Taney's opinion clearly implied that "the subject was one with which the federal government could not interfere."[15] Taney added:

> Any slave state had the right to guard itself . . . from the introduction of free negroes among its slaves, and that this right had not been surrendered by the adoption of the Constitution of the United States. . . .

Abolitionism, the movement to totally do away with slavery divided the country. The North and South were divided on how to deal with the difficult question of slavery. The South needed slave labor to produce its cotton. The North did not use slaves to produce its goods.

The negroes themselves had no constitutional rights in the matter.[16] Southern whites considered free Negroes a threat to the stability of slavery.

Taney continued,

> The African race in the United States even when free, are everywhere a degraded class, and exercise no political influence. The privileges they are allowed to enjoy, are accorded to them as a matter of kindness and benevolence rather than of right. They are the only class of persons who can be held as mere property, as slaves . . . They were not looked upon as citizens by the contracting parties who formed the Constitution . . .[17]

Taney believed that even if certain states provided legal rights and citizenship to blacks, they still did not have United States citizenship.

Taney's views about the social and legal position of Negroes in the United States were perfectly clear in 1832, twenty-five years before he wrote the majority opinion in the *Dred Scott* decision. He considered the Declaration of Independence irrelevant concerning the status of the Negro. He said:

> Our Declaration of Independence was drawn by a distinguished citizen of a slave-holding state [Thomas Jefferson of Virginia], and when it was asserted . . . 'that all men are created equal; that they are endowed by their Creator with certain inalienable rights; that among these are life, liberty and the pursuit of happiness . . .'—no one ever supposed that the African race in this country were entitled to the benefit of this declaration.[18]

Like all sons of Maryland tobacco plantation owners, Roger Taney had been raised with slaves and had accepted their condition as normal and right. There were slaves in every house in Maryland. And in every one of the colonies, slavery was recognized as legal. The New England colonies imported slaves from Africa, and the Southern colonies purchased them. Slave labor was the only labor in the South. It had become a part of their society.

In the early part of the nineteenth century in both the North and South, it was believed that the Negro was inferior. Nearly all northern cities denied Negroes the right to vote. In Massachusetts, Negroes were discouraged from settling there.

Between 1850 and 1860 Maryland had the greatest number of Negro slaves. Roger Taney hoped for their gradual emancipation, which was already underway in that state. But he felt it was the right of each state to handle the problem in its own way.[19]

By 1860, the number of slaveholders in the South had shrunk. In Virginia, North Carolina, Kentucky, and Tennessee, only one family in four owned slaves.[20] A strong religious tide swept the North, starting with the Quakers who had always opposed slavery. Today we know slavery was wrong and should never have happened.

In the summer of 1818, Jacob Gruber, a Methodist minister from Pennsylvania, was preaching a sermon at a camp-meeting in Hagerstown, Maryland. About three thousand people, four hundred of them Negroes, attended. He said, "We Pennsylvanians think it strange . . . to read the . . . newspapers . . . and find—*For sale, a plantation, a house and lot, horses, cows, sheep, and hogs; also a number of negroes—men, women and children—some very valuable ones; also a pew in such and such a church.* In this inhuman traffic and cruel trade the most tender ties are torn asunder, the nearest connections broken."[21]

Gruber had cast a slur upon Maryland by claiming that his state of Pennsylvania was the more civilized. For preaching this sermon, Jacob Gruber was indicted by the Grand Jury of Washington County, Maryland, on the charge that he intended "unlawfully and maliciously, to incite the slaves who heard him to insurrection and rebellion for the disturbance of the peace of the State."[22]

At Gruber's request, the case was removed to Frederick. Roger Taney was hired to defend Gruber before a slaveholding jury and slaveholding judges. Taney said,

> No man can be prosecuted for preaching the articles of his religious creed; . . . Therefore, the reverend gentleman, whose cause I am now advocating, cannot be liable to persecution . . . for the sermon mentioned. . . . He is accused of an attempt to excite . . . insurrection among our slaves; . . . No slave-holder is allowed to be a minister of that [Methodist] church. Their preachers are accustomed in their sermons, to speak of the injustice and oppressions of slavery. . . . Mr. Gruber did not go to the slaves: they came to him.[23]

The jury retired. A few minutes later, they brought in the verdict. Not guilty.

One other event that occurred at that time also bore great significance for the nation. And Roger Taney was to make reference to it thirty-five years later in the *Dred Scott* decision. The first serious clash between the North and South, slavery and antislavery interests, occurred in 1819 and 1820. By the end of 1818, the Union was made up of eleven free states and eleven slave states. The population in the North was greater than in the South, and thus there were more Northerners in the House of Representatives. Southern leaders felt strongly that the number of free and slave states should remain balanced so that the South would be equal to the North in the Senate. Maine was about to become a state and certain to be a free one; Missouri, on the other hand, was certain to be a slave state if admitted. A debate began in Congress over the admission of Missouri to the Union. Antislavery forces were urging that Missouri be admitted only on the condition that slavery be outlawed there. The proslavery people objected to any such condition. The issue was discussed and agitated over in the newspapers and at mass meetings. After a lot of political maneuvering, Congress passed, on March 3, 1820, a bill that became known as the Missouri Compromise. According to its terms, Maine was to be admitted as a free state and Missouri a slave state. The compromise was that slavery was to be forever prohibited below the southern boundary of Missouri. It seemed a fair solution at the time. And it put the slavery question to rest for awhile.

By 1831, when Taney became Attorney General and a member of the Jackson cabinet, Congress and the entire nation had got caught up in a political war with the Second Bank of the United States. Because of the "Bank War," as it was called, Taney was to give up his Attorney General post three years later and become Jackson's Acting Secretary of the Treasury.

William Dunne, Secretary of the Treasury, was instructed by Jackson to withdraw all government deposits from the second Bank after Nicholas Biddle, the bank's president restricted national credit. He refused. This time Jackson demanded his resignation. Dunne again refused. An angry Jackson wrote Dunne the following note: "I feel myself constrained to notify you that your further services . . . are no longer required."[24]

President Jackson knew that Roger Taney supported and

stood behind him regarding the Second Bank situation, so he immediately appointed Taney to fill the vacancy left by Dunne. Jackson wrote Van Buren: "Taney accepted, resigning the Attorney General's office and unites with me heart in hand . . . the business of the Treasury is progressing as though Mr. Dunne had never been born."[25]

Jackson ordered Taney to withdraw government deposits from the bank's branches. Nicholas Biddle, who knew he had lost, began winding up the bank's affairs. Three days after his appointment as Secretary of the Treasury, Taney announced that government funds would be deposited into state-chartered banks in Boston, New York, Baltimore, and Philadelphia. Nine days later, eleven more state banks were selected for deposits. "It has made the currency more sound and healthful,"[26] Taney wrote to a friend.

Taney's position as Secretary of the Treasury had been criticized by some of his friends in Frederick. They called him unfit for the office and indifferent to money matters. It was true that Taney had never spared money when it was needed for his family or charity, but he never spent beyond his income. "I did not hoard money but I never went into debt," Taney said in his defense, ". . . and while I lived there [Frederick] I never had a dispute with a merchant or mechanic about his bill."[27]

Jackson was being attacked for dismissing Dunne and assuming the sole responsibility for disposing of government money. Taney was criticized as nothing more than a "pliant instrument of Jackson . . . one of those . . . who literally crawled in their own slime to the footstool of Executive favor."[28]

In June of 1834, President Jackson sent Roger Taney's name to the Senate for formal confirmation as Secretary of the Treasury. The next day Taney was rejected. No debate. There were too many supporters of the United States Bank in the Senate. It was said he had "brought the country to a state of financial ruin and that he lacked intelligence, honesty and ability to deal with financial matters, that he was so weak as to be the mere tool of the man under whom he served."[29]

Taney had no choice but to resign. On the twenty-fifth of June, he wrote Jackson: "I cannot . . . take my final leave . . . without returning my cordial thanks for the many and continued proofs of kindness and confidence which I have received at your hands . . ."[30] Jackson replied: " I feel that I owe you a debt of gratitude and regard. . . . The plan of financial policy . . . and its beneficial effects on the currency of the country . . . will be . . . more than an adequate compensation for the . . . injustice to which you have now been subjected . . ."[31]

Taney's deposit system had been working smoothly. He felt a sense of victory, not defeat. He was proud of his accomplishments in the nine months he had served as Secretary of the Treasury. A few days after he left the post, Samuel Thomson, an acquaintance from Baltimore who had worked at the New York Customs House, sent Taney two boxes of Taney's favorite long, black cigars. The now former Secretary of the Treasury thanked Thomson: "I cannot accept the cigars . . . as a present. . . . It has been a fixed rule with me to accept of no present . . . from any one the amount of whose compensation for a public service depended on the department over which I had presided. . . . I will be glad to keep them . . . and must ask . . . you to say how much they are worth, that I may send you the money."[32]

Mr. Thomson answered: "You will oblige me much by accepting . . . of the trifle now in your possession as a mark of my respect for your great private worth and invaluable public services. . . . If your fine feelings and independent spirit will not allow this, then either return the cigars or enclose me $10."[33] Taney kept the cigars, sent Thomson $10, and even paid the postage.

Taney returned to Baltimore in a barouche (a four-wheeled carriage) pulled by four gray horses and accompanied by several hundred people on horseback. He was hailed by cheering crowds. Many public dinners were held in his honor in Baltimore and other Maryland cities. Of course, he could not attend all of them. One invitation he gladly accepted, though, was as the guest of honor at a dinner in his old hometown of Frederick, on the sixth of August, 1834.

That day bugles sounded and cannons roared. Frederick residents rushed to their windows to wave. Others lined the streets to cheer the return of their local hero. Taney gave a short speech at the hotel and then proceeded to the courthouse yard followed by a marching band and several hundred people. About twenty tables had been set up for the gala reception in Taney's honor. There followed many toasts and more cheers. After the final toast was proposed, Taney rose to address the crowd of applauding friends and supporters "untroubled by the sense of panic which so often paralyzed his best efforts on the platform."[34]

His speech was simple and clear. He explained the issues of the Bank War in words that the farmers in the audience could understand. Taney concluded his speech with a final warning against establishing another national bank anywhere for any purpose:

Yield but an inch, and you will be driven to the
wall . . . and instead of the rich inheritance of liberty
which you received from your fathers, you will
bequeath to your descendants, slavery and
chains—the worst of slavery, that of submission to
the will of a cold, heartless, soulless, vindictive
monied corporation . . . And in conclusion . . . I beg
leave of you to offer the following toast: Frederick
County—Rich in the productions of its soil—but
richer far in the patriotism and manly independence
of its citizens.[35]

During the three years Taney had served as Attorney
General of the United States, he had been able to maintain a
small law practice as well. But, as Secretary of the Treasury, he
had had to abandon it completely. When his government
position ended, he had to start all over again. One would
think that the prestige Taney had enjoyed in government
service would have enabled him to reestablish himself in a
short time. But this was definitely not the case. He had made
too many enemies during the Bank War. Attempts to recover
his law practice were blocked from many sides.

At the same time Taney continued to suffer from bad
colds and attacks of arthritis, which made his every movement
quite painful. He wrote Jackson: "In the vindictive spirit
which prevails here towards me . . . I am obliged to give strict
attention to my professional concerns, in order to sustain
myself against the influence which is seeking to prevent me
from reestablishing myself in my former practice."[36]

The President hated to see Taney struggle with such
difficulty. He missed him in Washington. Taney's name had
been mentioned as a possible vice-presidential candidate along
with Martin Van Buren who was being groomed to succeed
Jackson. But Taney was not in a financial position to run nor

did he have an interest in another political office in Washington.

Administration leaders continued to call on him for advice and assistance on various matters. Van Buren stopped in Baltimore to visit Taney and reported back to Jackson that Taney's health was improving and that he promised to return soon to Washington. "Remember," Jackson wrote Taney, "I have a bed and room for you."[37]

And in just a few short years, Roger Brooke Taney did return—to become the Chief Justice of the United States.

4

"To Stand Before His Uplifted Hand"

Associate Justice Gabriel Duvall from Maryland had been sitting on the bench for twenty-three years. He was getting old and was often absent from the Court. He was described as "the oldest-looking man on the bench . . . his head . . . white as a snow bank . . . so deaf as to be unable to participate in conversation."[1] The death of his wife of almost forty years and the illnesses of old age may have been factors in his decision to retire in 1835. When he heard that President Jackson intended to appoint his fellow Marylander Roger Taney to succeed him, he agreed at once to step down. He left the Court in January.

Taney remembered Duvall well. He had tried his very first case before Judge Duvall as a young lawyer in Annapolis. He later recalled that Duvall's manner was "kind and encouraging even if he had a grave face and dignified deportment."[2]

Jackson sent Taney's name to the Senate for confirmation as an Associate Justice of the Supreme Court the day after Duvall resigned in January of 1835. The nomination was discussed but no action was taken. The Senate was still bristling over Taney's role in the Bank War. There was a lot of opposition to his appointment. The last day of the Senate session arrived. Still no word. Jackson, working late at the Capitol signing bills, was becoming anxious. In the Senate, at shortly past midnight, Daniel Webster finally called for a vote. Taney was narrowly defeated: twenty-four to twenty-one. The Senate secretary notified Jackson who "threw down his pen, roared that it was more than an hour past twelve . . . [he] would receive no more messages from the scoundrels, . . . stalked out of the building."[3]

Early in the summer of 1835, just three months before his eightieth birthday, Chief Justice John Marshall died. But no one was nominated to fill his place until the end of that year. Many names were mentioned as Marshall's replacement: names like Justice Joseph Story, to "succeed to the chair of his beloved chief,"[4] and Senator Daniel Webster were mentioned. Jackson, however, felt that Webster was "devoid of truth, honor, and patriotism."[5]

On December 28, 1835, President Andrew Jackson once again sent Roger Brooke Taney's name to the Senate for confirmation as Chief Justice of the United States. There was hardly any criticism of Taney's legal ability, but it was said that his work as Secretary of the Treasury would "damn him to everlasting fame."[6]

No action was taken for more than two months. Delaware senator John Clayton presented a petition signed by members of the Baltimore bar urging Taney's confirmation.

Meanwhile, Taney was busy arguing a case in Annapolis

When President Jackson sent Roger Taney's name to the Senate for confirmation as Chief Justice, there was hardly any criticism of his legal ability.

and not too worried about his prospects. He knew that Jackson, Van Buren, and others would defend his interests in Washington. Then Francis Scott Key learned from Clayton that Taney's nomination was finally to be taken up by the Senate. Key knew that Taney was tied up with an important case in Annapolis, so he wrote to the two Georgia senators asking them to try and postpone action on the nomination for three days.

Upon hearing of this, Taney was alarmed. He was afraid that his Senate opponents would make use of Key's letter to defeat his nomination. It was one thing to tell trusted friends that he didn't want the confirmation hearing hastened because of a case pending before the Maryland legislature, but quite another to have a letter circulated requesting the postponement of his nomination in order for him to argue a case. Luckily, though, Key's attempt at playing politics had no effect whatever.

An angry Taney wrote Van Buren: "I have no desire that my nomination would be postponed an hour on account of my engagements at Annapolis."[7] Then, Virginia senator John Tyler (who was to become the tenth president of the United States in 1841) abruptly resigned over disagreements with Jackson, after serving nine years in the Senate. On March 14, 1836, Jacksonian Democrat William Rives replaced Tyler. The Jackson forces now had a majority in the Senate. It looked good for Taney. Confirmation came soon after: twenty-nine to fifteen. The nation had a new Chief Justice!

A leading Washington newspaper wrote: "Mr. Taney is beloved by all who know him . . . he never had an enemy . . . his principles are of the most liberal."[8] In Annapolis, congratulations starting pouring in. On March 17, Taney wrote to the President expressing his "deep gratitude for the way Jackson had always supported him, culminating in his appointment to the one office under the federal government which he had ever wished to attain."[9] Taney replied to a letter of congratulations from an old friend in Frederick: "My political battles are over and I must devote myself to the calm but high duties of the station with which I am honored."[10] And a former law student of Taney's from Frederick, wrote: "...I am proud that you will be now the very head itself of a profession you have always loved and honored."[11]

His nomination now confirmed, Taney could hardly continue arguing his case in the Maryland House of Delegates. He handed his notes over to an associate and took a seat with the other citizens in the audience. It was the last case in which he appeared as an attorney.

On March 28, 1836, at eleven in the morning family and friends and members of the bar gathered in the courtroom of the Capitol. There, Roger Brooke Taney was sworn in as the fifth Chief Justice of the United States and Presiding Judge for the 4th Circuit, which included Delaware, Maryland, and Virginia, which was added in 1842.

The Judiciary Act of 1789 required that, in addition to their work in Washington, D.C., each Supreme Court Justice had to preside over a circuit, or district court. Each Justice was required to spend part of the year sitting as a trial judge in the circuit courts that were located within his geographical district. Each Justice also had to be familiar with the laws of at least one of the states in his circuit.

Roger Taney held circuit court each year in Baltimore, Maryland, Richmond, Virginia and New Castle and Dover, Delaware. This involved some hardship for Taney. The trip to Delaware was strenuous. Taney had to ride by stagecoach more than three hundred miles over rough country roads. He

On March 28, 1836, Roger Brooke Taney was sworn in as the fifth Chief Justice of the United States. The coat hook that Taney hung his judicial robe on is shown here.

estimated that he must have traveled about four hundred fifty-eight miles each year.[12] One of the other Justices reported that he had traveled ten thousand miles.[13]

The Justices complained bitterly about the difficult and demanding travel. It was unreasonable to require elderly men, after serving in the Supreme Court, to have to ride so many miles through rough country to preside over local courts when they should be in Washington. They were even willing to take a cut in salary if only Congress would appoint separate district judges. But Congress refused. One senator even suggested that the Justices would be influenced by the president if they were to stay too long in Washington.

Circuit riding was important, however, because it provided opportunities for the Justices to learn about local conditions and local law. And it was much easier for a judge to travel to the community than for the parties and their witnesses to travel to Washington.

On April 8, 1836, Roger Taney's official duties as a presiding judge for the 4th circuit began in Baltimore. It was said that he presided "in a manner courteous but firm, which won the approval of the public . . ."[14]

At the opening of the Supreme Court term, the new Chief Justice took his center seat on the bench for the first time. It was three months short of his sixtieth birthday. Taney impressed spectators as "tall, narrow of face, with clear black hair and an elasticity of step . . . beneath his official robe he wore ordinary democratic garb, instead of the knee breeches customarily donned by [Marshall]. . . . He was the first Chief Justice . . . to depart from precedent and give judgment in trousers."[15] Taney swore in more presidents than any other Chief Justice. They included Van Buren, Harrison, Polk, Taylor, Pierce, Buchanan, and Lincoln.

Two months later, Taney administered the oath of office to Martin Van Buren, the first of seven presidents who were "to stand before his uplifted hand."[16] Van Buren had just been elected the eighth president of the United States. Former president Andrew Jackson, seventy years old and in failing health, attended the inauguration, saying "nothing should detain him from witnessing the august spectacle at the Capitol . . . and he wanted to see one citizen . . . now sworn in by another citizen, who . . . was now made Chief Justice of the United States."[17]

The old practice of Justices rooming and eating their meals together continued during Taney's early years on the Court. Because of this close living arrangement, the Justices were able to discuss the work of the Court at all hours. But, as living conditions improved, the Justices began to live apart, although this did not seem to change their relationships with each other at all. The bachelor Justices were able to find accommodations for about $17 a week, while the married Justices had to pay around $40.[18]

Over the years the Justices moved from one boarding house to another. Taney first lived at Elliott's Boarding House on Pennsylvania Avenue and two years later moved to Mrs. Turner's. He wrote to his son-in-law James Mason Campbell, "I have not been fortunate in boarding arrangements . . . My room is very good . . . but all the rest of the house is more comfortless than you can well imagine."[19] Washington itself in the 1840s was a city of "dust in summer and mud holes in winter with everyone taking as a matter of course the cows, geese and swine that roamed loose in the streets."[20]

As Chief Justice, Taney had to participate in many social functions. He attended formal dinners, laid cornerstones, introduced friends to foreign diplomats, expressed

Roger Taney (left) swore in more presidents than any other Chief Justice. He is seen here administering the oath of office to President James Buchanan on March 4, 1857.

condolences upon the deaths of prominent people, even signed his name for autograph collectors. He performed all of these duties with a warmth and graciousness that resulted in many long-lasting friendships.

In the normal course of events, though, it was customary for the Justices to spend the early part of the morning in the study, reflection, and writing of opinions. At eleven o'clock in the morning they would meet to hear arguments and would adjourn at four in the afternoon to spend their time at leisure until after dinner. Then they would meet again at seven for a conference, which could be long and tedious.

In spite of Taney's frail health and occasional absences, his output was greater than his colleagues. During the twenty-eight years he served as Chief Justice, Taney wrote two hundred eighty-one opinions, speaking for the majority in two hundred and sixty cases, writing dissents in fourteen, and concurrences in only seven.[21]

The Taney Court was made up of independent thinkers who often had conflicting views. (At the first session in 1836, there were seven members, five of whom had been appointed by President Jackson; within a year, two more were added. One was appointed by Jackson and the other by Van Buren, to make a total of nine.) Sometimes they could not even agree on internal matters.

Along with the court clerk, an important member of the Court was the reporter of decisions. His job was to transcribe the Court's decisions from their authors to print so that those decisions could be made available to the public. But some of the Justices were never satisfied with this method or sometimes with the reporter. They claimed there were errors or omissions in the final results.[22]

In one instance, Taney was not successful at convincing

the other Justices about the selection of a reporter. In the beginning of the 1843 Court term, four of the Justices were unhappy with Court Reporter Richard Peters' work. They voted to appoint a new reporter, Benjamin C. Howard from Taney's home state of Maryland. Taney had wanted Peters to stay on, but he was outvoted. The Justices overruled their Chief again in 1861. This time Benjamin Howard decided to run for governor of Maryland, so he had to resign from the Court. When he was defeated, he tried to get his old job back. Taney said yes but was outvoted again. Jeremiah Black became the court reporter. One wonders whether Taney thought this aspect of the Chief Justice's role was as important as judging itself.[23]

In one of Taney's first and most famous Supreme Court opinions, he spoke for the people in a case involving a clash between private rights and state powers: the Charles River Bridge controversy. "The interest of the public must . . . always be regarded as the main object,"[24] Taney said. Owners of the Charles River toll bridge, operating under a charter from the state of Massachusetts, claimed that the state could not allow another company to open the Warren Bridge nearby. Chief Justice Taney ruled that Massachusetts *did* have the power to approve construction of the Warren Bridge, which would serve the people of Boston. "While the rights of private property are sacredly guarded . . . we must not forget that the community also have rights, and that the happiness and well being of every citizen depends on their faithful preservation."[25]

Taney's opinion received high praise from one Democratic magazine. "It is a most able document," they wrote, "he [Taney] pursued his unbroken chain of clear, logical reasoning, spreads light all around. . . . [T]he present

Chief Justice escaped from irrelevant matter with as much ease as Judge Marshall."[26]

Even as Taney began his career as Chief Justice, soon-to-be significant conditions were developing around the country. In the South, people had been investing more and more in Negroes, who then became their slaves for life. Slaves were used for the production of major crops such as tobacco and cotton. Meanwhile, the North had been industrializing and had no need for slaves. Over the years sharp contrasts developed between these two sections of the country.

When Taney had defended Methodist minister Jacob Gruber in Frederick in 1818, many Southerners admitted then that "serious problems grew out of their peculiar institution."[27] A few had freed their slaves, only to find that the now-free slaves were not able to care for themselves. Although the Supreme Court tried to avoid issues about slavery as long as possible, controversies surrounding the cultural and economic division in the country found their way there nevertheless.[28]

Perhaps as an omen of things to come, another case came up during Taney's first term as Chief Justice: the *Amistad Case* of 1841. Spanish slave merchants had brought with them from Africa a cargo of Negroes who had been illegally sold in Havana, Cuba. Their new owners ordered them shipped to another Cuban port. While sailing from Havana, the Negroes revolted, killed the captain, and ordered the ship to sail back to Africa. Instead, they headed for the United States. The *Amistad* was captured off the coast of Connecticut, and the Negroes sought asylum in the United States as free men. The Van Buren administration wanted to return them to their Spanish masters.

The case was brought before the Supreme Court and

aroused much excited discussion everywhere. Northern feeling was for the Negroes. Southerners were for the ship owners. The Taney Court decided in favor of the Negroes. Taney said that the Negroes were subject to the laws of the state where they happened to be, in this case, Connecticut, an antislavery, or free state. With growing friction between the North and the South, Taney did not think the federal government should interfere. He still felt that those states unwilling to abolish slavery should deal with it as they saw fit.[29]

Other problems were also creating friction. Slaves would escape from their masters in the South and flee to the North. When the Constitution was drafted in 1787, representatives from the South had demanded guaranteed property rights for fugitive slaves. So a compromise had been made: "No person held to service or labor in one State, under the laws thereof, escaping into another, shall, in consequence of any law or regulation therein, be discharged from such service or labor, but shall be delivered up on claim of the party to whom such service or labor may be due."[30] The Constitution had thus provided, by law, for the return of runaway slaves to their owners. The Constitution had become the defender of the rights of slave owners.

Six years later, the Fugitive Slave Law of 1793, effective in all states, provided that fugitive slaves should be returned to their masters. Pennsylvania, for instance, had strict laws concerning the rights of Negroes within its borders. Enforcement of the Fugitive Slave Law depended upon the cooperation of state officers, however, who were in many instances against slavery. They would allow escaped slaves to easily enter the state. Southern slave owners, of course, criticized this practice. In 1826, the Pennsylvania legislature passed a law "to prevent the taking of negroes not legally owned . . . but to prescribe a manner in which lawful owners might make their claims effective."[31] An escaped slave was to be brought before a judge where his or her owner had to show proof of ownership. If the judge was convinced the claim was authentic, he would issue a certificate authorizing the Negro's removal from the state.

In a case that reached the Supreme Court in 1842, during the administration of President John Tyler, the constitutionality of this law was challenged. *Prigg* v. *Pennsylvania* concerned a Negro woman and her children who had escaped from their owner in Maryland—a slave state—and fled to Pennsylvania—a free state. The owner hired Edward Prigg, a professional slave catcher, to get them back. In accordance with Pennsylvania law, Prigg brought the slave family before a judge, but the judge refused to authorize their removal. Prigg took the family back to Maryland anyway.

Prigg was indicted for kidnapping by the state of Pennsylvania. After friendly negotiation between the two states, Maryland and Pennsylvania agreed that the case should be brought before the final decider of constitutional questions—the Supreme Court of the United States.

In his decision, Chief Justice Taney said, "The language used in the Constitution . . . contains no words prohibiting the several states from passing laws. . . . [T]he right of the master, therefore, to seize his fugitive slave, is the law of each state."[32] He agreed that the Pennsylvania law was unconstitutional. Taney added, "The legal rights of the master over the slave . . . were entitled to protection from the federal and state governments by virtue of the legal and compact nature of the Constitution. . . . Existing law dealt with the negro in his traditionally degraded condition. . . . It was the function of judges to apply the law, and not to teach morality or preach religion."[33]

The decision did not sit well with the North or the South. The North resented the fact that it could not enforce laws regarding escaped slaves. The South was told that their laws aiding the recapture of slaves were unconstitutional; that the states to which their slaves had fled were not obliged to give assistance. The Supreme Court was criticized from all sides. There were "distant rumblings of disaster which grew louder and louder until the storm burst upon the country in the form of . . . civil war."[34]

Meanwhile, on the political front, William Henry Harrison had won the presidential election of 1840 by a landslide. At the inauguration, on March 4, 1841, Chief Justice Taney administered the oath of office to the new president. The day was unusually cold, but Harrison refused to wear a jacket. He caught a cold, which turned into pneumonia; he died exactly one month later. Vice President John Tyler then became president, the first to succeed to the presidency because of the death of an elected president. He was sworn in by Taney and became the tenth president of the United States.

Tyler, who had a mind of his own, was unpopular within his own party. The Whigs' plan to run the country through a friendly military gentleman like Harrison had been ruined, and Tyler became a president without a party. The Whigs now hoped that no Supreme Court Justices would die until a new Whig president was elected. When Chief Justice Taney suffered a serious illness, one of the Justices wrote to his son, "His [Taney's] constitution is . . . feeble and broken; but I trust and hope that he will be spared until times assume a better aspect."[35]

Taney recovered. In the next election, in 1844, the Democrats put up forty-nine-year-old James Knox Polk, with the blessings of Andrew Jackson, as their candidate for the next president. The Whigs' candidate was Henry Clay, but the Whigs once more went down in defeat. Taney sent congratulations to the victorious Polk: "...your triumphant success gives me increased confidence in the intelligence, firmness and virtue of the American people. . . . I need not say with what pleasure I shall again meet you in Washington, and see you entering upon the high station to which you have been so honorably called."[36]

Taney had continued to correspond with his old friend Andrew Jackson. On New Year's Day, Taney paid an official call on Polk at the presidential mansion. He wrote to Jackson: "...Where I have so often seen you; and in the rooms where I was accustomed to find you; and perhaps I looked at them with the more pleasure because I know they are soon to be occupied by one of your most firm and faithful friends."[37]

Over these years, the issue of slavery continued to come up. In a case that reached the court in 1851, the federal government's power to ban the extension of slavery was defined. A Kentucky resident who owned slaves trained them as musicians. He hired them out to an agent/coach who got them bookings at public amusement spots. One of the places where they entertained was in the state of Ohio, a free state. No attempt was made to interfere with the agent's control over the slaves while they were in Ohio. Eventually, they were returned to their owner in Kentucky.

Some time later, however, the slaves escaped and were taken across the Ohio River by a man named Strader. Strader was arrested and prosecuted according to a Kentucky law that required punishment for helping slaves escape from their masters. Strader's defense was that the Negroes were not slaves because they had already been taken into the free state of Ohio.

Taney disagreed with Strader's defense. In his opinion he declared:

> Every state has an undoubted right to determine the status, or domestic and social condition of the persons domiciled within its territory . . . there is nothing in the Constitution of the United States that can in any degree control the law of Kentucky upon this subject. And the condition of the negroes, therefore, as to freedom or slavery, after their return, depended altogether upon the laws of that state, and could not be influenced by the laws of Ohio. It was exclusively in the power of Kentucky to determine for itself whether their employment in another State should or should not make them free on their return.[38]

Because Strader had been aiding the slaves when he helped them escape, he therefore was subject to punishment.

On the political front, just as President Tyler was leaving office, Congress approved the annexation of Texas. The following year, the United States and Mexico were at odds over the geographical boundary between their two countries. The war with Mexico that followed resulted in the annexation by the United States of a large part of the southwest. No sooner had the territory been acquired than Congress had to decide which parts could be admitted to the Union. After much debate, it enacted the Compromise of 1850, which had the following provisions:

- California to be admitted as a free state.
- New Mexico and Utah to be organized as territories that could decide for themselves their status as slave or free states.
- Slave trade prohibited in the District of Columbia.
- Passage of a more stringent fugitive slave law.
- Texas to be paid $10 million to relinquish much of its western territory to the federal government.

Voices in both the North and the South were in favor of accepting the 1850 Compromise. They wanted to put the question of slavery behind them and proceed with the business of the nation. But the slavery issue would not go away. In 1854, a young senator from Illinois named Stephen Douglas introduced the Kansas-Nebraska Act. It would enable the settlers in those states to decide for themselves whether or not to allow slavery within their boundaries.[39] Congress passed the Kansas-Nebraska Act, which angered Northerners. The evils of slavery were debated at town meetings in every northern state.

Chief Justice Taney also continued to preside over the Supreme Court as changes occurred in its makeup. In 1854, for example, five of the nine Justices came from slaveholding states. By the year 1856, Chief Justice Roger Taney was held in high esteem by his colleagues on the Supreme Court and had become a respected national figure. Henry Clay, who had opposed Taney's nomination in the Senate, admitted that he had done him an injustice. "I am now convinced," said Clay, "that a better appointment could not have been made."[40]

In 1856 Roger Brooke Taney was seventy-nine years old. If he had died or retired at that time, his reputation as a great Supreme Court Justice would have remained secure. But a case that had been making its way up through the lower courts to the Supreme Court was to change all that. It concerned a Negro slave by the name of Dred Scott.

5

"Can Any of You Help Me in My Day of Trial?"

The nation was short-tempered over slavery. And the Missouri Compromise of 1850 had not helped. Senator Stephen Douglas's Kansas-Nebraska Act of 1854 opened slavery in states closed by the Missouri Compromise. The slavery question was revived once again. There were violent border incidents. Domestic harmony had to be restored. Someone had the idea that the *Dred Scott* case might be the test case that could restore peace on the home front.

By the time the case reached the Supreme Court, more issues than just the free or slave status of one Negro were involved. The questions were clear: Had four years' residence in free territory made Dred Scott a free man? Is a free Negro considered a citizen of the United States according to the Constitution? And, if so, could he sue in a United States Court? Is the Missouri Compromise constitutional? Should the expansion of slavery be allowed?

One slave by the name of Dred Scott thus became the focal point of the nation's destiny. Born "Sam" in Virginia around 1795, he took the name "Dred Scott" as he grew older. He had been a slave to the Blows of Virginia. When Peter Blow died in 1832, Dred, then about thirty-seven years old, was sold to Dr. John Emerson, an Army surgeon from St. Louis, Missouri. Dr. Emerson's duties required him to leave the slave state of Missouri and travel to the free states of Illinois and present-day Wisconsin, and Scott went with him. While there, Scott married Harriett Robinson, the slave of a federal agent. They eventually had two daughters, Eliza and Lizzie.

Emerson returned with the Scotts to Missouri in 1834 and died soon after. He left his estate, which included Dred, Harriet, Lizzie, and Eliza to his wife, Irene.

The Scotts, claiming to be free because they had lived in the free state of Illinois, filed charges against the widow Emerson for holding them as slaves, and for assault, claiming she had "beat, bruised and ill-treated them."[1] Dred Scott tried in vain to persuade Mrs. Emerson to let him find work for wages so that he could buy freedom for his family. She refused. This denial of what he felt were his rights convinced Scott to take his case to a Missouri court. On April 6, 1846, Dred Scott's ten-year quest for freedom began.

The state court had often granted freedom to slaves taken by their masters to free states or territories. The Dred Scott case appeared simple enough. But complications arose. There were postponements, delays. Four years passed. At last, the case reached the Missouri Circuit, or District Court. The petition was denied, but, because of a technicality, the judge granted a motion for a new trial, which took place in early

Dred Scott, his wife Harriet, and their two daughters, Eliza and Lizzie, were at the center of a heated debate that would decide the fate of slavery.

January, 1850. This time, Scott won his case and was declared free. Mrs. Emerson appealed to the Missouri Supreme Court.

In 1851, the Taney Court, in the *Strader* v. *Graham* case, had ruled that whatever status a Negro had enjoyed outside of one state, his return to his home state made him subject to that state's laws. The Court had refused to review a decision of the Kentucky Court of Appeals that a short trip by some Kentucky slaves to the free state of Ohio did not make them free. The laws of Kentucky, not Ohio, determined their status once they had returned to Kentucky.

On March 22, 1852, the Missouri Supreme Court ruled that Dred Scott was still a slave according to Missouri law. Mrs. Emerson had won. The judge said "slavery had been in the providence of God, who makes the evil passions of men subservient to His own glory, a means of placing that unhappy race within the pale of civilized nations."[2]

It did not look good for Scott. Irene Emerson remarried, moved to Springfield, Massachusetts, and left the matter in the hands of her brother, John Sanford. The Taney Court received the official record of *Dred Scott* v. *Sandford* (Sanford's name was misspelled by the Court clerk and was never corrected) in 1854, at the same time as the Kansas-Nebraska Act was being discussed and debated in Congress.

Prominent St. Louis attorney Montgomery Blair agreed to represent Scott without a fee. Blair, an able and experienced lawyer, became strongly committed to Scott and his cause. But who would pay the court costs? Gamaliel Bailey, the editor of the Republican newspaper *National Era* promised to raise money to pay for incidental expenses which ". . . amounted to the nominal sum of $154.68."[3] Dred Scott, with the help of the Blow family, circulated this appeal:

I have no money to pay anybody at Washington to speak for me. My fellow-men, can any of you help me in my day of trial? Will nobody speak for me at Washington, even without hope of other reward than the blessings of a poor black man and his family? I do not know. I can only pray that some good heart will be moved by pity to do that for me which I cannot do for myself; and that if the right is on my side it may be so declared by the high court to which I have appealed.[4]

Late in December of 1854, the Supreme Court received the case but because it was late in the term, it was to be carried over to the following year. But the Court calendar became so crowded that oral arguments in the case could not be heard until February 1856, over a year later. Montgomery Blair was growing impatient. So was his client, Dred Scott, who was now in the ninth year of his pursuit of freedom.

Of the nine Justices on the Supreme Court—Roger Taney, James M. Wayne, John McLean, John Catron, Peter V. Daniel, Robert C. Grier, Samuel Nelson, John A. Campbell, and Benjamin R. Curtis—five—Taney, Wayne, Daniel, Catron, and Campbell—were Southern, proslavery Democrats. Blair could hardly have been confident of success. He knew of Taney's past decisions in cases similar to Dred Scott's; for example, *Strader* v. *Graham*, in which a slave was denied freedom. In court, Blair could hardly help noticing that Taney's age and chronic physical afflictions had taken their toll. One reporter noted that "Taney had a sinister expression suited to the role of malevolent villain."[5]

The progress of the case of Dred Scott was reviewed in an atmosphere of great political excitement. The Kansas-Nebraska Act had passed the Senate and the Republican Party was emerging. There was a presidential campaign coming up in 1856. Congress was debating about slavery in the territories. In the beginning, the *Dred Scott* case had focused only on Scott's quest for freedom and nothing else. Blair reaffirmed the ruling of the lower court that Scott had limited citizenship, qualifying him to bring suit in a federal court. But now new issues were raised. Sanford's lawyers claimed that Scott as a Negro, was not a citizen and therefore could not sue in federal court. Then they made their big mistake! They brought up the territorial issue and argued that the Missouri Compromise was unconstitutional. After the arguments ended, the Justices were too divided in their opinions. The only decision they reached was to delay any action until the next court term and after the upcoming presidential election.

Arguments for both sides resumed in December 1856 and lasted for four days. Then began the long wait for the Court's decision. Only a handful of people believed that Dred Scott would come out of this a free man. Montgomery Blair wrote to Martin Van Buren: "It seems to be the impression that the Court will be adverse to my client and to the power of Congress over the Territories."[6]

Almost two months passed before the Supreme Court began its second round of conferences on Dred Scott's fate, finally beginning in February 1857. The Court was again divided on the issue of Negro citizenship. Also the Southern majority on the Court decided to take up the issue of whether the congressional restriction on slavery, set up by the Missouri Compromise, was constitutional. They apparently hoped that a firm judicial decision would end the political controversy over slavery in the territories. The southern slave owners then tried to persuade the northern Democratic Justices to decide with them.

On February 3, President-elect James Buchanan wrote

Justice John Catron of Tennessee asking if the Court was going to give its opinion on the *Dred Scott* case before his inauguration on March 4. Catron replied nine days later that the majority had decided to give an opinion on whether the Missouri Compromise was constitutional. He then asked Buchanan to "drop Grier [a Northern Democratic Justice from Pennsylvania] a line, saying how necessary it is . . . to settle the agitation by an affirmative decision . . . one way or the other."[7]

On February 23, in reply to an urgent note from Buchanan, Catron reported: "I want Grier speeded."[8] That same day, Grier, unaware of Catron's involvement, replied to a letter from Buchanan: "On conversation with the Chief Justice, I have agreed to concur with him."[9] It looked like three Southern Justices, one compliant Northern Justice, and the president-elect had secretly made a pawn of Dred Scott in a game of judicial politics.

The nation wanted the slavery problem solved faster than constitutional processes could act on it. In the center of the tide sweeping the nation stood Chief Justice Taney. In his own conscience, he was opposed to slavery, but, by virtue of his high office, he was sworn to uphold the Constitution as he saw it. Taney did not always agree with the Constitution. However, he felt he had to interpret it as it was written, not as he would like to have seen it written.

George Washington and Thomas Jefferson had also owned slaves but "neither thought it was right for a man to own another man, as he owned a horse or dog."[10] As early as 1776, they and other wise Southerners and Northerners were convinced that slavery was a morally bad system. Thomas Jefferson had wanted to include a paragraph denouncing slavery in the Declaration of Independence, but the other committee members voted him down. It would have caused a split at the time, so Jefferson left it out. In 1776, most people were persuaded that there was money to be made in the slave system. By 1857, however, many had begun to doubt that slavery was all that profitable.

The opinion that Taney wrote in the *Dred Scott* decision reflected his Southern upbringing. He tried to preserve the culture and independence of the South that he felt were worth saving, even though he knew it meant the preservation of slavery on the one hand and civil war on the other.[11]

"In the opinion of the Court," Taney wrote in the majority opinion on Dred Scott:

> the legislation and histories of the times, and the language used in the Declaration of Independence, show, that neither the class of persons who had been imported as slaves, nor their descendants, whether they had become free or not, were then acknowledged as part of the people, nor intended to be included in the general words used in that memorable instrument. It is difficult at this day to realize the state of public opinion in relation to that unfortunate race, which prevailed in the civilized and enlightened portions of the world at the time of the Declaration of Independence, and when the Constitution of the United States was framed and adopted.

He went on,

> They had for more than a century before been regarded as beings of an inferior order; and altogether unfit to associate with the white race, either in social or political relations; and so far inferior, that they had no rights which the white man was bound to respect.

In conclusion, Taney wrote:

Chief Justice Taney wrote the *Dred Scott* Decision on this desk. The opinion that Taney wrote reflected his Southern upbringing. The desk is currently on display at the Taney house in Frederick, Maryland.

> Upon the whole, therefore, it is the judgment of this
> Court . . . that the plaintiff in error is not a citizen of
> Missouri, in the sense in which that word is used in
> the Constitution and that the Circuit Court of the
> United States, for that reason, had no jurisdiction in
> the case, and could give no judgment in it. Its
> judgment for the defendant must, consequently, be
> reversed, and a mandate issued directing the suit to be
> dismissed for want of jurisdiction.[12]

The Supreme Court, in a seven-to-two decision, had ruled
that Dred Scott was not a citizen of the United States and was
not entitled to be one because Negroes were of an inferior
order. But they didn't stop there. Slaves were property, they
said, and property had to be protected whether it be a slave in
Georgia or a mule in Vermont. According to the
Constitution, Congress had no power over property rights in
the states, and therefore had no power to abolish slavery. And,
since the Missouri Compromise interfered with property
rights, it was declared unconstitutional.

The *Dred Scott* case backfired on those who had hoped to
stop the controversy that threatened to destroy the nation. For
the past ten years, those opposed to slavery had been hacking
away at the high status of the Supreme Court. They had now
succeeded. It seemed as if the prestige the Court had enjoyed
up to now had been wrecked. Many were shocked that the
Chief Justice had actually said that the Negro had no rights
the white man was bound to respect. Horace Greeley, an
ardent abolitionist, wrote an editorial the day after the
decision was announced: "The decision was entitled only to
the weight to be given to the judgment of . . . persons in any
Washington barroom. . . . What he [Taney] had to say had
been still more feeble than his voice."[13]

And another leading New York newspaper wrote:

> The moment the Supreme Judicial Court becomes a court of injustice . . . the moment its claim to obedience ceases . . . the decision . . . is not a mistake [but] a deliberate willful perversion, for a particular purpose, and that purpose the sanction . . . of human slavery. If the people obey this decision they disobey God.[14]

The Court term ended. Taney was criticized from all sides. He did not reply to any of his critics. He maintained the belief that the *Dred Scott* decision would contribute to the welfare of both Negroes and whites.[15] But it only added fuel to the bitter controversy between the North and the South. The Chief Justice had allowed himself to get involved in a political argument when he had only needed to make a judicial decision.

President James Buchanan agreed with the decision of the Supreme Court. He felt that the Constitution clearly protected citizens' property. He viewed slaves as property and believed the federal government could do nothing about it.[16] "Slavery was the south's problem," he said, "and neither the north nor the President had any right to interfere. Taney hates slavery as I do, but this is a matter beyond the personal feelings of the President and the Chief Justice. . . . The matter is settled, the Constitution shall be upheld."[17]

Some time after the *Dred Scott* decision, Taney wrote a letter to former President Franklin Pierce. The letter showed Taney's confidence in his decision:

This photograph of Roger Brooke Taney, was presented to his daughter, Alice Taney, in March 1855. The inscription read: "A token of love for Alice Carroll Taney from her affectionate father." It was signed R.B. Taney, dated March, 1855. The photo is in the Taney house, Frederick, MD.

At my time of life when my end must be near, I should
have rejoiced to find that the irritating strifes of this
world were over, and that I was about to depart in peace
with all men. . . . I have an abiding confidence that this
act of my judicial life will stand the test of time and the
sober judgment of the country.[18]

Even though the decision resulted in Dred Scott's defeat,
his freedom was secured three months later. The Emerson
family turned the Scotts over to Scott's former owners, the
Blows, who freed them on May 26, 1857. Unhappily, the
newly freed slave did not get much chance to enjoy his
newfound freedom, nor did he live to see slavery abolished.
Dred and Harriet Scott and their two daughters continued
living in St. Louis, Missouri. Dred got a job working as a
porter at Barnum's Hotel. Harriet worked as a laundress.
Sixteen months later, on September 17, 1858, Dred died of
tuberculosis. He was sixty-three. Dred Scott's nemesis in the
case, John Sanford, died in an insane asylum two months after
the reading of the decision.

Newspaper accounts of Scott's death were brief. Some
editors reflected on the significance of his day in court. "In
ages to come," wrote the editor of the *New York Herald,*
"Dred Scott and the decision which bears his name will be
familiar words in the mouth of the ranting demagogue in
rostrum and pulpit, and of the student of political history."[19]

No doubt Roger Brooke Taney and his brethren on the
Supreme Court meant to protect Southern interests and to curb
the power of the North despite its greater population. The Taney
Court had attempted unsuccessfully to determine national policy.
But the northern majorities and sectional ill will had escalated to
the point that they could not be restrained by the Supreme

Court. To many, the *Dred Scott* decision was the most "unwelcome decision in the history of the court."[20]

When what the majority of the people regard as a great wrong exists and they are told there is nothing to be done about it in a peaceful way, it is certain that something violent will happen. And it did. The North and the South moved toward a national calamity in 1861. A calamity known as the Civil War. And, before the slavery question would be resolved, over 780,000 Americans would lose their lives.[21]

6

"Our Constitution Is Color-blind"

Chief Justice Taney never regretted his decision. Soon after Republican Abraham Lincoln was elected president in 1860, there were rumors that Taney would resign while Democratic president James Buchanan was still in office in order to assure that a Democrat would be appointed Chief Justice.

But the rumors were false. Taney, at eighty-five, could give no serious thought to resigning. He needed his salary to live on. He had to support his daughters, Sophia and semi-invalid Ellen. He was still treated by his colleagues with respect, but in public he was "detested as a man who drew his pay from the Federal Government while lending sympathy to its enemies."[1] The *Dred Scott* case had wrecked Taney's reputation.

Taney presided over a Court now without much influence. The Lincoln administration ignored him. On

February 16, 1863, Taney wrote a letter to Secretary of the Treasury Salmon Chase complaining that a "3% deduction from his salary for income tax was unconstitutional."[2] He did not even get a reply. Because Taney had written the major opinion in the *Dred Scott* case, he had been singled out for attack. A leading New York newspaper had this to say: "That decision [Dred Scott] wrong as it was, did not spring from a corrupt or malignant heart. It came . . . from a sincere desire to compose . . . sectional discord. But yet it was nonetheless an act of supreme folly . . ."[3] Most damaging of all to him was the charge that he had deliberately meant to degrade Negroes. Taney was simply following the eighteenth-century frame of mind that prevailed when the Constitution was adopted.

The *Dred Scott* case and the whole question of slavery was made obsolete by the passage of the Thirteenth Amendment right after the Civil War ended, late in 1865.

> Neither slavery nor involuntary servitude, except as a punishment for crime whereof the party shall have been duly convicted, shall exist within the United States or any place subject to their jurisdiction.[4]

Taney's ruling about citizenship was resolved with the passage of the Fourteenth Amendment three years later:

> All persons born or naturalized in the United States and subject to the jurisdiction thereof, are citizens of the United States and of the State wherein they reside. No state shall make/or enforce any law which shall abridge the privileges or immunities of citizens of the United States; nor shall any State deprive any person of life, liberty, or property, without due process of law; nor deny to any person within its jurisdiction the equal protection of the laws.[5]

This bust of Chief Justice Roger Brooke Taney by Augustus
Saint-Gaudens is on view in the Robing Room of the old
Supreme Court chamber.

Both constitutional amendments gave the government the authority to protect the rights of *all* citizens.

Negroes could no longer be denied the right to sue in a federal court. Five cases actually reached the Supreme Court by 1883. Known as the civil rights cases, they involved issues such as exclusion from a hotel dining room in Topeka, Kansas, a hotel in Missouri, an opera house in New York City, theaters in San Francisco, a ladies' car on a train in Tennessee. Negroes, at last considered citizens, wanted to enjoy all the privileges of citizenship.

The Supreme Court tended to narrowly interpret the Civil War amendments. The Court's narrow-mindedness was evident with regard to the Civil Rights Act of 1875, which it declared unconstitutional. The Act prohibited racial discrimination in "inns, public conveyances, and places of public amusement"[6] but limited federal efforts to protect Negroes from private discrimination. The Act also cast constitutional doubts on Congress' ability to pass laws in the area of civil rights. Doubts which would not be resolved until the Civil Rights Act of 1964.

To enforce segregation by color beginning in the 1880s, the Southern states developed a system of laws and customs that separated negroes from whites. These were known as the Jim Crow Laws, named after a Negro relegated to an inferior social status. The laws covered schools, theaters, restaurants, hotels, and public transportation.

A test case to challenge the Jim Crow Laws came before the Supreme Court in 1896. A Louisiana Negro named Homer Plessy had purchased a ticket for the short train ride from New Orleans to Covington. When he was asked by the conductor to move to the "colored only" section of the coach, he refused. He was arrested.

The Court found that:

> separate but equal accommodations . . . [did not stamp] the colored race with a badge of inferiority . . . in this instance the white race is property, in the same sense that a right of action, or of inheritance, is property. . . . If he be a white man and assigned to a colored coach, he may have his action for damages against the company for being deprived of his so-called property. Upon the other hand, if he be a colored man and be so assigned, he has been deprived of no property, since he is not lawfully entitled to the reputation of being a white man. . . . If the civil and political right of both races be equal one cannot be inferior to the other. . . . If one race be inferior to the other socially, the Constitution cannot put them upon the same plane.[7]

Plessy lost his case. Justice John Marshall Harlan had written the only dissenting opinion in the earlier civil rights cases, and he also dissented in the Plessy decision. "The judgment this day rendered will in time prove to be quite as pernicious as the decision made by this tribunal in the *Dred Scott* case," he wrote. "It seems that we have yet, in some of the states, a dominant race, a superior class of citizens, which assumes to regulate the enjoyment of civil rights, common to all citizens, upon the basis of race."[8]

Harlan also later wrote on the same subject, "our Constitution is color-blind. . . . In respect of civil rights, all citizens are equal before the law."[9]

With the *Plessy* v. *Ferguson* decision, state-ordered segregation invaded every aspect of daily life in the South. Negroes had to continue to ride in separate streetcars; use separate waiting rooms, toilets, water fountains, parks, theaters, mental hospitals, and prisons; and attend segregated schools. Negroes were still regarded as inferior to whites. They couldn't even live on the same streets as whites.

The "separate but equal" doctrine put in place by *Plessy* v. *Ferguson* remained a rule of law for many years. In the 1890s races could be segregated if equal facilities were provided. The main question was, however: Could separate facilities be equal? This question would not be answered until the second half of the twentieth century, when the *Brown* v. *Board of Education* case in Topeka, Kansas, would force a historic reversal of the *Plessy* v. *Ferguson* decision.

From 1896 on, the "separate but equal" doctrine remained the law of the land. Because of this law many states and the District of Columbia continued to operate segregated school systems. In 1951, however, things began to change. In that year, Oliver Brown of Topeka, Kansas, sued that city's school board because his eight-year-old daughter Linda had to cross railroad yards to catch a bus that would take her to a black school twenty-one blocks from her home. Brown wanted Linda to attend the white school that was only five blocks from their home. His lawyers argued that segregation in the schools violated the Fourteenth Amendment. Three federal judges found that the schools were substantially equal and ruled against Brown. They said that the *Plessy* decision controlled the case.

So Brown took his case to the Supreme Court. The first arguments were heard in December 1952. Chief Justice Earl Warren, on May 17, 1954, read the unanimous opinion of the Court: "In the field of public education the doctrine of 'separate but equal' has no place. Separate educational facilities are inherently unequal."[10] The Court had ruled that segregation in public schools deprived children of "the equal protection of the laws under the Fourteenth Amendment."[11]

In 1955 the Court added, "Desegregation would now proceed with all deliberate speed."[12]

In 1957, the Supreme Court directed school officials in the twenty-one states with segregated classrooms to desegregate. Most states obeyed the order. Arkansas did not. In 1958, Governor Orval Faubus, with the help of the Arkansas National Guard, tried to prevent black students from entering an all-white high school in Little Rock. Only after the Supreme Court demanded the state stop resisting were the students admitted. The racial crisis in Little Rock prompted *The New York Times* to write "This was a time when national unities were again imperiled by a Supreme Court judgment."[13]

Still, by 1964, less than 2 percent of black students in Southern states were attending desegregated schools.[14] President Lyndon Johnson, a Southerner, managed to get a Civil Rights Act through Congress that year. No person, because of race, could be excluded from any facility that is open to the public, nor be discriminated against in employment. The country was finally moving in the direction of eliminating the racial discrimination that had been a part of American life for so long.

By the middle of the twentieth century, Roger Brooke Taney had come to be generally recognized as one of the country's great Supreme Court Justices. Many historians believed he had received unfair criticism at the time of the *Dred Scott* decision in 1857. In September 1931, Chief Justice Charles Evans Hughes, the son of an abolitionist minister, unveiled a bust of Taney in Frederick, Maryland. "Taney's career," Hughes said, "should have been influenced by his most important contributions, not by the *Dred Scott* case

This bust of Roger Brooke Taney was unveiled by Chief Justice Charles Evans Hughes in September 1931, in front of the courthouse in Frederick, Maryland. Even as late as 1964, the negative effects of the *Dred Scott* decision were still being felt. Less than 2 percent of black students in Southern states were attending desegregated schools.

alone. . . . Taney was a man of invincible spirit . . . he was a great Chief Justice."[15]

Turmoil arises when a country confronts new dangers and new ideas about the meaning of freedom. The Supreme Court continues to "hold up the goal of equal rights as an ideal for society to strive to achieve."[16] It has been the "ultimate guardian of the rights we enjoy and the obligations we accept as a free people. [It] remains the voice of the Constitution."[17]

Chronology

1777—Roger Brooke Taney is born on March 17 in Calvert County, Maryland.

1792–1795—Taney attends Dickinson College, Carlisle, Pennsylvania.

1796–1799—Taney studies law in Annapolis, Maryland.

1799—Taney is admitted to the Annapolis Bar; elected to Maryland House of Delegates.

1801—Taney moves to Frederick, Maryland, to begin law practice. Admitted to the Frederick Bar.

1806—Taney marries Anne Phebe Charlton Key.

1819—Taney defends Jacob Gruber.

1827—Taney becomes Attorney General of Maryland.

1831—Taney becomes Attorney General of the United States.

1833—President Andrew Jackson names Taney Acting Secretary of the Treasury.

1834—Nomination of Taney for Secretary of the Treasury is rejected by the Senate.

1835—Nomination of Taney for Associate Justice of the Supreme Court is rejected by the Senate.

1836—President Jackson nominates Roger Brooke Taney for Chief Justice of the United States; nomination confirmed by Senate.

1837—*Charles River Bridge* v. *Warren Bridge*.

1841—*United States* v. *Schooner Amistad*

1842—*Prigg* v. *Pennsylvania.*

1851—*Strader* v. *Graham.*

1855—Taney's wife and daughter die in yellow fever epidemic.

1857—*Dred Scott* v. *Sandford.*

1864—Roger Brooke Taney dies on October 12 in Washington, D.C.

Chapter Notes

Chapter 1

1. *New York Daily Tribune*, Horace Greeley editorial, March 26, 1859, p. 4.

2. William H. Rehnquist. *The Supreme Court. How It Was, How It Is* (New York: William Morrow, 1987), p. 150.

3. Charles Warren, *The Supreme Court in United States History*. Vol. I (Boston: Little, Brown, 1926), pp. 694–695.

4. From 1844–1917, opening day of the Supreme Court term occurred on the second Monday in December. Since 1917 the term has begun the first Monday in October.

5. Carl Brent Swisher, *Roger B. Taney (New York: The Macmillan Company, 1935), p. 500.*

6. Donald Bruce Johnson, comp., *National Party Platforms Volume I 1840–1956* Democratic Platform of 1856. (Urbana, Ill.: University of Illinois Press, 1978), p. 25.

7. Samuel Eliot Morison, *The Oxford History of the American People, Volume II, 1789–1877 (New York: Penguin Books, 1972), p. 363.*

8. Until 1933, Inauguration Day was March 4. In 1933, the 20th Amendment to the Constitution changed the date to January 20.

9. Morison, p. 363.

10. *Inaugural Addresses of the Presidents of the United States from George Washington 1789 to Richard Milhous Nixon 1969* (Washington, D.C.: United States Government Printing Office, 1969), p. 112. (James Buchanan's Inaugural Address March 4, 1857.)

11. Northerner in favor of slavery in the South before or during the Civil War.

12. *New York Daily Tribune*, Horace Greeley editorial, March 5, 1857.

13. *Guide to the U.S. Supreme Court* (Washington, D.C.: Congressional Quarterly, Inc., 1979), p. 761.

14. Harriet Martineau, "Retrospect of Western Travel," Vol. I. London: 1838, p. 165, as quoted in *The Supreme Court Chamber, 1810–1860.* (Washington, D.C.: The United States Senate Commission on Art. n.d.).

15. *Dred Scott* v. *Sandford,* 19 Howard 393 (1857).

16. From the Latin word "niger" meaning black, *negro* inferred that black, as opposed to white, was bad, evil, ugly, inferior. In the 1950s, the term *colored* was more commonly used; with the rebirth and resurgence of the civil rights movement of the 1960s, *black* came into frequent use. Today, to reflect a new dignity and a sense of nationality to people of African descent, the most commonly used term is *African-American.*

17. *Dred Scott* v. *Sandford.*

18. Ibid.

Chapter 2

1. Carl Brent Swisher, *Roger B. Taney* (New York: Macmillan Company, 1935), p. 9.

2. Samuel Tyler, *Memoir of Roger Brooke Taney, LL.D.* (Baltimore: John Murphy & Co., 1872), pp. 26–27.

3. Ibid., p. 34.

4. Ibid., p. 28.

5. Ibid., p. 36.

6. Ibid.

7. Judge Edward S. Delaplaine, "Taney Notebook Displayed in Area Library," *The Frederick Post*, October 13, 1986, p. A8.

8. Ibid.

9. Ibid., p. A9.

10. Ibid.

11. Tyler, p. 51.

12. Ibid., p. 52.

13. Ibid., p. 53.

14. Ibid., p. 54.

15. Ibid., p. 56.

16. Walker Lewis, *Without Fear or Favor* (Boston: Houghton Mifflin, 1965), p. 30.

17. Not until 1898 were bar examinations required in Maryland. Permission to practice law was granted or not granted individually to each applicant.

18. Tyler, pp. 75–76.

19. Ibid., pp. 77–78.

20. Judge Edward S. Delaplaine, "Taney Goes to Frederick After Re-Election Try Fails." *The Frederick Post*, October 17, 1986, p. A-10.

21. Tyler, p. 94.

22. Ibid., p. 95.

23. Ibid., p. 101.

24. Judge Edward S. Delaplaine, "Taney-Key Marriage," *The Frederick News*, April 1, 1972, p. 2.

25. Lewis, p. 44.

Chapter 3

1. Carl Brent Swisher, *Roger B. Taney* (New York: Macmillan Company, 1935), p. 108.

2. Ibid., p. 109.

3. F. J. Nelson. *The Frederick News*, April 11, 1893, Editorial.

4. John E. Semmes, *John H. B. Latrobe and His Times*, pp. 344–345, as quoted in Swisher, p. 117.

5. Gordon Carruth, *Encyclopedia of American Facts and Dates*, (New York: HarperCollins Publishers, 1993), p. 178.

6. Swisher, p. 142.

7. Key to Taney, June 14, 1831, as quoted in Samuel Tyler, *Memoir of Roger Brooke Taney, LL.D.* (Baltimore: John Murphy & Co., 1872), pp. 170–171.

8. Jackson to Van Buren, June 23, 1831, as quoted in Swisher, p. 141.

9. *Baltimore Republican*, July 1, 1831, as quoted in Swisher, p. 141.

10. Walker Lewis, *Without Fear or Favor* (Boston: Houghton, Mifflin, 1965), p. 124.

11. Modern equivalents were supplied by the United States Department of Labor, Bureau of Labor Statistics, New York.

12. Swisher, p. 147.

13. Ibid.

14. *Official Opinions of the Attorney General*, as quoted in Swisher, p. 150.

15. Ibid., p. 151.

16. Ibid., p. 153.

17. Ibid., p. 154.

18. Ibid., p. 158.

19. Lewis, p. 360.

20. Ibid., p. 362.

21. Tyler, p. 126.

22. Ibid., pp. 126–127.

23. Ibid., pp. 128–129.

24. Jackson to Duane, September 23, 1833, as quoted in Swisher, p. 234.

25. Jackson to Van Buren, September 23, 1833, as quoted in Swisher, p. 234.

26. Taney to Beall, October 15, 1833, as quoted in Swisher, p. 239.

27. Taney to Beall, September 29, 1833, as quoted in Swisher, p. 237.

28. Swisher, p. 287.

29. Ibid.

30. Taney to Jackson, June 25, 1834, as quoted in Tyler, pp. 221–222.

31. Jackson to Taney, June 25, 1834, as quoted in Tyler, p. 223.

32. Taney to Samuel Thomson, June 28, 1834, as quoted in Tyler, p. 237.

33. Ibid.

34. Swisher, p. 295.

35. *Taney's Speech in the Courthouse Yard at the Public Festival Given to Him by the Jackson Republicans of Frederick County, Maryland*, August 6, 1834.

36. Taney to Jackson, October 20, 1834, as quoted in Swisher, p. 306.

37. Jackson to Taney, November 8, 1834, as quoted in Swisher, p. 308.

Chapter 4

1. Clare Cushman, ed., *The Supreme Court Justices: Illustrated Biographies, 1789–1993* (Washington, D.C.: Congressional Quarterly, Inc., 1993), p. 85.

2. Ibid., p. 83.

3. Carl Brent Swisher. *Roger Brooke Taney* (New York: Macmillan Company, 1935), p. 314.

4. Ibid., p. 316.

5. *Washington Globe*, August 21, 1835, as quoted in Swisher, p. 317.

6. Allan Nevins, ed., *Diary of Philip Home*, p. 164, as quoted in Swisher, p. 317.

7. Taney to Van Buren, March 15, 1836. Van Buren MSS, as quoted in Swisher, p. 321.

8. *Washington Globe*, April 2, 1836, as quoted in Swisher, p. 323.

9. Swisher, p. 323.

10. Taney to Beall, March 23, 1836, as quoted in Swisher, p. 324.

11. James Dixon to Taney, March 17, 1836, as quoted in Swisher, p. 324.

12. Taney to John Forsyth, September 9, 1838. Miscellaneous Letters, Department of State, as quoted in Swisher, p. 354.

13. Swisher, pp. 354–355.

14. Ibid., p. 357.

15. "The Supreme Court," *United States Magazine and Democratic Review*, January 1838, as quoted in Swisher, p. 359.

16. Swisher, p. 357.

17. *Richmond Enquirer*, March 13, 1837, as quoted in Swisher, pp. 336–337.

18. W. T. Carroll to Smith Thompson, December 15, 1837, as quoted in Swisher, p. 353.

19. Taney to J. Mason Campbell, February 8, 1839, as quoted in Swisher, p. 353.

20. Walker Lewis, *Without Fear or Favor* (Boston: Houghton Mifflin, 1965), p. 277.

21. Robert J. Steamer, *Chief Justice, Leadership and the Supreme Court* (Columbia, S.C.: University of South Carolina Press, 1986), p. 106.

22. Ibid.

23. Ibid.

24. *Charles River Bridge* v. *Warren Bridge*, 11 Peters 420 (1837).

25. Ibid.

26. "The Supreme Court," *United States Magazine and Democratic Review*, January 1838, as quoted in Swisher, p. 376.

27. Swisher, p. 414.

28. Ibid., p. 415.

29. Ibid., p. 418.

30. The Constitution of the United States, Article IV, Section 2.

31. Swisher, pp. 420–421.

32. Ibid., p. 423.

33. Ibid.

34. Ibid., p. 425.

35. J. Story to W. W. Story, January 30, 1844, as quoted in Swisher, p. 431.

36. Taney to Polk, November 20, 1844, as quoted in Swisher, p. 435.

37. Taney to Jackson, January 1, 1845, as quoted in Swisher, p. 436.

38. *Strader* v. *Graham*, 10 Howard 82 (1851).

39. William H. Rehnquist, *The Supreme Court. How It Was, How It Is* (New York: William Morrow, 1987), p. 137.

40. Charles W. Smith, *Roger B. Taney: Jacksonian Jurist* (New York: Da Capo Press, 1973), p. 15.

Chapter 5

1. Kenneth M. Stampp, *America in 1857* (New York: Oxford University Press, 1990), p. 83.

2. Ibid., p. 85.

3. Ibid., p. 86.

4. Don E. Fehrenbacher, *Slavery, Law and Politics* (New York: Oxford University Press, 1981), p. 147.

5. Stampp, p. 87.

6. Blair to Van Buren, February 5, 1857, as quoted in Stampp, p. 89.

7. Stampp, p. 92.

8. Catron to Buchanan, February 23, 1857, as quoted in Stampp, p. 92.

9. Grier to Buchanan, February 23, 1857, as quoted in Stampp, p. 92.

10. Gerard W. Johnson, *The Supreme Court* (New York: William Morrow, 1962), p. 76.

11. Carl Brent Swisher, *Roger B. Taney* (New York: Macmillan Company, 1935), p. 505.

12. *Dred Scott* v. *Sandford,* 19 Howard 393 (1857).

13. *New York Daily Tribune,* Horace Greeley editorial, March 7, 1857.

14. *New York Independent,* March 9, 1857.

15. Swisher, p. 518.

16. David R. Collins, *James Buchanan 15th President of the United States.* (Ada, Okla.: Garrett Educational Corporation, 1990), p. 116.

17. Ibid.

18. Taney to Pierce, August 29, 1857, as quoted in Swisher, pp. 518–519.

19. Fehrenbacher, p. 295.

20. Swisher, p. 523.

21. *The World Almanac and Book of Facts 1994* (Mahwah, N.J.: Funk and Wagnalls, 1993), p. 708.

Chapter 6

1. Don Fehrenbacher, *Slavery, Law, and Politics* (New York: Oxford University Press, 1981), p. 296.

2. Taney to Chase, as quoted in Carl Brent Swisher, *Roger B. Taney* (New York: Macmillan, 1935), pp. 568–569.

3. *The New York Times*, October 13, 1864, as quoted in Fehrenbacher, p. 298.

4. Constitution of the United States, Amendment XIII, Section 1. Ratified December 6, 1865.

5. Constitution of the United States, Amendment XIV, Section 1. Ratified July 9, 1868.

6. Kermit L. Hall, ed., *Oxford Companion to the Supreme Court of the United States* (New York: Oxford University Press, 1992), p. 149.

7. *Plessy* v. *Ferguson*, 163 U.S. 537 (1896).

8. Ibid.

9. Mary Ann Harrell and Burnett Anderson, *Equal Justice Under Law* (Washington, D.C.: Supreme Court Historical Society, 1988), p. 60.

10. *Brown* v. *Board of Education of Topeka*, 347 U.S. 483 (1954).

11. Ibid.

12. Harrell and Anderson, p. 100.

13. Fehrenbacher, p. 306.

14. Elder Witt, advisory editor, *The Supreme Court A to Z* (Washington, D.C.: Congressional Quarterly Inc., 1993), p. 79.

15. Don Fehrenbacher, *The Dred Scott Case, Its Significance in American Law and Politics* (New York: Oxford University Press, 1978), p. 590.

16. Ibid., p. 81.

17. Harrell and Anderson, p. 104.

Where To Write

The Supreme Court Historical Society
111 Second Street N.E.
Washington, DC 20002

For original copies of the Dred Scott Decision *of 1857 and the Judiciary Act of 1789, which established the federal court system.*

The Home and Museum of Chief Justice Taney
Attention: Elizabeth Speciale
121 South Bentz Street
Frederick, MD 21701

The Taney house is open to the public from April through October, Saturday 10 AM to 4 PM and Sunday 1 PM to 4 PM.

Tourism Council of Frederick County
19 East Church Street
Frederick, MD 21701
Attention: Beth Finneyfrock

Frederick Historical Society
24 East Church Street
Frederick, MD 21701
Attention: Angie Brosius, Head Librarian

The Maryland Historical Society
Museum and Library of Maryland History
201 West Monument Street
Baltimore, MD 21201

Glossary

abolitionist—A person opposed to slavery.

amendment—A measure added to the Constitution since it was adopted in 1787.

appeal—To take a case to a higher court.

argument—Oral presentation of a case made by an attorney.

attorney general—Head of the Justice Department and member of the president's cabinet who serves as his legal adviser; the chief law enforcement officer of the United States. The Attorney General has been a Cabinet member since 1789 when George Washington was president. The Justice Department was not established until 1870 when Ulysses S. Grant was president.

bill— A measure proposed for action before a legislative body.

Bill of Rights—The first ten amendments to the Constitution. From hundreds of suggestions from the states, James Madison created a list of seventeen amendments, which he presented to the House of Representatives. The Senate whittled the list down to twelve, of which ten were ratified by the states on December 15, 1791.

brethren—Up to 1981, Supreme Court Justices were all men; they were called "brethren," which means "brothers."

cabinet—A group appointed by the president to head specific executive departments and to serve as advisers.

case—A suit or some other law action.

Chief Justice—The highest judicial officer of the United States, appointed for a life term by the president with the consent of the Senate. He presides over sessions of the Supreme Court.

circuit court—A court that sits at two or more places within one judicial district.

circuit riding—Required by the Judiciary Act of 1789, it served to establish contact between the people and the federal judiciary.

citizen—A native or naturalized member of a state as defined in the Fourteenth Amendment.

Civil Rights Amendments—Laws passed by Congress to guarantee the rights of Negroes after the Civil War.

civil war—A war between opposing groups of citizens of the same country. The American Civil War took place from 1861 to 1865.

clerk of the court—The person who keeps the Court running smoothly. The office was established in 1790. William T. Carroll of Maryland was the clerk of the Taney Court.

conferences—Meetings where the Supreme Court Justices grant or deny judicial review and decide cases. Conferences are conducted in complete secrecy. The Chief Justice presides over the conference.

Congress of the United States—The legislative branch of the federal government consisting of the Senate and House of Representatives. Congress introduces laws, regulates commerce, coins money, establishes post offices, maintains armed forces, and declares war. The first Congress met in 1789.

Constitution—The basic law establishing the framework of government. It establishes the relationship between the people and their government. The Constitution went into effect March 4, 1789; it has 27 Amendments. It is the supreme law of the land.

decision—The court's judgment when a case is settled.

Declaration of Independence—A basic statement of American beliefs made to declare independence of the American colonies from England. It was drafted by Thomas Jefferson, John Adams, Benjamin Franklin, Roger Sherman, and Robert Livingston and adopted on July 4, 1776.

Democrat—One of two major political parties. Democrats believe that the federal government should be actively involved in correcting social inequality. Thomas Jefferson, Andrew Jackson, and Roger Taney were Democrats.

docket—A special calendar on which a case is scheduled.

due process—The right to fair treatment.

emancipation—The process of setting people free from slavery.

federal government—A type of central government.

Fourteenth Amendment—A part of the Constitution that defines citizenship and forbids states to deprive any person of life, liberty, or property without due process.

House of Representatives—Members of Congress who represent each state. Some states have more than one member depending on their population. A representative must be over twenty-five years old, a United States citizen for at least seven years, and a resident of the state that elects him or her. The House can impeach federal officials, originate revenue bills, and elect the president if no candidate gets a majority in the electoral college. In 1789, there were 65 members; today, there are 435 members.

Jim Crow Laws—A law adopted by Southern states to enforce segregation of whites and Negroes in the 1880s.

judge—A government official who has the power to decide cases in a court of law. A Supreme Court government official is called a Justice.

judgment of the court—The official decision of the Court based on the full review of a case. The Court can uphold, modify, or reverse a decision made in a lower court. It may also void a lower court decision. If this occurs, the Court may send the case back to the lower court to be reconsidered; the Court's opinion guides the lower court on the principles of law it should consider.

Judiciary Act of 1789—A law passed by the first Congress to establish a Federal Court System.

kitchen cabinet—An informal group of close friends and personal advisers to the president. The term originated when Andrew Jackson was president (1828–1836) and a group met in the kitchen of the White House.

Marshal of the Court—The officer who calls the Supreme Court to order. He cries "Oyez, Oyez, Oyez!" (old French word for "hear ye"). He is the Court's general manager, paymaster, and chief security officer. The position was created in 1867. Before then, his duties were performed by the Clerk or the Marshal of the district in which the court was located. In Taney's day, the twelve men who served as Marshal of the District of Columbia also served as Marshal of the Court.

monopoly—Having exclusive control, making it impossible or unprofitable for others to take over.

opinion—A written explanation by a judge about the legal principles on which a court decision is based.

plaintiff in error—A person who complains or sues in a personal action and is named on the record.

president—The Chief Executive of the United States. A key official in the American system of government.

Republican—The more conservative of the two major political parties organized (1854) out of the Whig Party, which hated slavery. John C. Frémont, the Republican Party's first presidential candidate, was defeated by Democrat James Buchanan in 1856. Abraham Lincoln was a Republican.

segregation—Separation of whites and Negroes in public and private facilities.

Senate—It has one hundred members, two from each state. A senator must be over thirty years old, a United States citizen for at least nine years, and a resident of the state that elects him or her. The Senate has the power to advise and consent on appointments of important government officials, including ambassadors and federal judges.

sitting—To be in session for official business.

slave—A person considered as property.

suit—An action against a person in a court of law.

Supreme Court of the United States—The highest court in the land. It interprets the meaning of the Constitution.

term—When the court is in session.

test case—The first test of major legislation. Also refers to any landmark case, such as *Dred Scott* v. *Sandford.*

Thirteenth Amendment—A part of the Constitution that forbids slavery anywhere in the United States.

unconstitutional—Not according to the wording and principles of the Constitution of the United States.

veto—To refuse to admit or approve. A power vested in the president to prevent the enactment of measures passed by a legislature.

Further Reading

Aaseng, Nathan. *Great Justices of the Supreme Court.* Minneapolis, Minn.: Oliver Press, 1992.

Friedman, Leon. *The Supreme Court.* New York: Chelsea House Publishers, 1987.

Harrison, Maureen, and Steve Gilbert. *Landmark Decisions of the United States Supreme Court.* Beverly Hills, Calif.: Excellent Books, 1991.

Herda, D.J. *The Dred Scott Case: Slavery and Citizenship.* Hillside, N.J.: Enslow Publishers, 1994.

Lawson, Don. *Landmark Supreme Court Cases.* Hillside, N.J.: Enslow Publishers, 1987.

Osinski, Alice. *Andrew Jackson.* Chicago: Children's Press, 1987.

Patrick, John J. *The Young Oxford Companion to the Supreme Court of the United States.* New York: Oxford University Press, 1993.

Richie, Donald A. *U.S. Constitution.* New York: Chelsea House, 1989.

The Supreme Court A to Z. Washington, D.C.: Congressional Quarterly Inc., 1993.

Weiss, Ann E. *The Supreme Court.* Hillside, N.J.: Enslow Publishers, 1987.

Index